Careers in Music

John Westcombe

**Published in association
with NAME**

Heinemann Educational Publishers
Halley Court, Jordan Hill, Oxford OX2 8EJ
a division of Reed Educational & Professional Publishing Ltd

OXFORD FLORENCE PRAGUE MADRID ATHENS
MELBOURNE AUCKLAND KUALA LUMPUR SINGAPORE TOKYO
IBADAN NAIROBI KAMPALA JOHANNESBURG GABORONE
PORTSMOUTH NH (USA) CHICAGO MEXICO CITY SAO PAULO

First published as *A Handbook on Careers in Music* 1986

© MANA, 1986

This fully revised edition published 1997

© John Westcombe, 1997

00 99 98 97
10 9 8 7 6 5 4 3 2 1

British Library Cataloguing in Publication Data

A catalogue record for this book is available from the British Library

ISBN 0 435 80996 2

Designed by Jackie Hill
Cover illustration by Balvir Koura
Typeset by TechType, Abingdon, Oxon
Printed and bound by Biddles Ltd, Guildford

Acknowledgements
The publishers would like to thank the following for permission to
reproduce copyright material.

Chappell of Bond Street for the advertisement on p.82; City of
Birmingham Symphony Orchestra for the advertisement on p.70;
Eastern Arts Board for the advertisement on p.98; Higher Education
Funding Council for England for the extract on p.19 from *Subject
Overview Report: Music,* p.12; London Symphony Orchestra for the
advertisement on p.84; Mayking Multi-Media for the advertisement on
p.94; Andrew Peggie in *Music Scholar* (Rhinegold Publishing Ltd),
March 1996 for the extract on p.103; *Q* magazine for the
advertisement on p.72; Royal Northern College of Music for the
advertisement on p.92; The Stables for the advertisement on p.75.

The publishers have made every effort to trace copyright holders.
However, if any material has been incorrectly acknowledged, we would
be pleased to correct this at the earliest opportunity.

Contents

Preface

The first edition of *Careers in Music* was launched in 1986 by the Minister of State at the Department of Trade and Industry, following extensive consultation. It was published by the Music Advisers' National Association (MANA) with John Westcombe as chief writer and compiler. Many colleagues in the profession, the music business and the careers services gave generously of their time, then and more recently, in terms of both correspondence and visits. In this edition papers of the writing team and guest contributors have been revised and new sections have been added.

Heinemann Educational and the author express warm appreciation to MANA and individual contributors for waiving copyright on material.

This handbook should be directly helpful to school pupils and music students, as well as parents, staff and those embarking on a career. There are other helpful brochures published by, among others, the Incorporated Society of Musicians, but *Careers in Music* offers case studies and several other commentaries. In particular, it sets out some of the decision-making processes that all young musicians need to make. It then draws together encouraging information about the employability of musicians and places all this in a wider context.

It is clear that there are many fulfilling employment opportunities in the field of music and its performance and many are listed in this book, to show both the diversity and range. Formal music qualifications are not always necessary for many of them; not all of the posts are in London, nor even full-time.

Significant developments in music technology, provision of instrumental lessons in LEA-maintained schools, and the rise of specialist ensembles in the professional sector are but three factors contributing to changes in career patterns. Also, the solid fact remains that the music profession and related businesses contribute hugely to the UK's economy, particularly through exports, and music's ability to inspire devotion from those for whom it is not a career, as well as for those who have undertaken training, is undiminished.

Acknowledgements

Grateful thanks are due to:

MANA (now National Association of Music Educators – NAME)

The guest contributors (whose names appear after their papers)

The writers of the case studies

Members of the original and later writing teams: Maxwell Pryce, John Stephens, Michael Wearne, Pat Gane, David Howe

Paul, Cynthia and Alexander for their assistance in the final preparation of copy.

How to use this book

If you are a young person set on training in music and building a career in that area, you, and others with whom you will want to discuss your plans, should find useful directions in this book. There are also several careers based in and around music that do not have to be preceded by formal training in the subject, and in this book you are encouraged to explore various routes.

What's included?

You will find two main sections in this book. Part 1 outlines some facts and decisions to be made at 16, 18 and 21–2 about whether to continue education or find a job. Part 2 provides details about careers with an exclusive or strong musical component. In addition, it provides a series of case studies – largely of people in their twenties still making their way – to give you some idea of the feasibility of developing a career in music.

The discussions in Part 2 are usually divided into four sections: **the job**, **skills and abilities** required, **opportunities**, and **training and qualifications**. Lists of follow-up reading or contacts are also included. Please look carefully at the Contents page, and use it to cross-refer between topics; much advice is common to several areas of employment.

People with disabilities who have particular skills or an interest in music should be able to contemplate most jobs mentioned in this book. Access facilities are still variable, but improving, and Equal Opportunities legislation is keeping employers aware of responsibilities.

Several blind, hearing-impaired and wheelchair-bound musicians have achieved international success in performing and teaching.

For a detailed listing of courses and much other relevant data you should refer to the *Music Education Yearbook* (MEY). This is normally published each May, priced at about £14, by Rhinegold Publishing Ltd, 241 Shaftesbury Avenue, London WC2H 8EH (Book Sales, telephone 0171 333 1721). This most useful publication, and its comprehensive counterpart the *British Music Yearbook,* should be in your public library. They are mines of information.

Note

The advertisements and the log of vacant posts are real examples. However, all the vacancies will have been filled before the publication of this book.

1

Preparing for careers in music

The musician's place in the world of work

Education, training and employment

The government, backed by all major employment organizations, has stressed the need for lifetime learning core skills as part of an intended 'change in culture' in training. The five skills important in education and vital to employers are:

- communication
- problem-solving
- personal skills
- numeracy
- information technology.

All public examination courses should now include elements of these core skills. Musicians have many strengths in these areas to show to employers and admissions tutors. The chart on **page 4,** based on a meeting between a county's education staff and senior personnel officers, illustrates this clearly.

When considering career possibilities, you should talk to a wide variety of people. There are also some computer programs that can assist you in evaluating your own qualities and attributes, and which can tell you about the requirements of specific areas of employment. They should be available in schools or college careers libraries, as well as your local careers centre. Employers, both in the music profession and in the world of business, are becoming increasingly aware of the qualities young musicians can offer. If students have realistic ambitions, and recognize that there is a large part of the world of music, particularly in the aspects of business, about which they know little, and employers recognize that musicians develop attitudes which are highly valued outside it, musicians will continue to play a vital part in the life of this country.

Music and the economy

Music plays an important part in the economy of the UK – see also *The Value of Music* (**page 25**). The high quality of professional performances attracts foreign visitors and we sell recordings, instruments and music (and collect royalties) extensively abroad. A survey by British Invisibles showed that in a recent year music made net earnings for the UK of over £570 million, a major contribution to the balance of payments (the difference between exports and imports). It is also estimated that the VAT on the sale of new instruments and live performance ticket sales makes nearly £150 million annually for HM Treasury. Music is among the arts that have attracted a total of £82.8m, contributed by the Association for Business Sponsorship of the Arts (ABSA) in the financial year 1994–5.

There are several other important points to note.

- If the music industry ceased today, countless people in the electronics industry would be out of work tomorrow.
- Over 620,000 people work in the arts and cultural industries.
- In a recent year, nearly 5 million people attended classical concerts, and 2.6 million supported jazz events.

(Sources: ABSA, Arts Council of England)

You should be able to find a place somewhere in all this activity!

What are employers looking for	What music can give you
People who can:	
1 **Show a good basic education** *Essential for almost any job*	Music contains elements of Maths, Physics, History, Languages, Art, Drama, Movement and Religious Education
2 **Follow instructions** *Essential for almost any job*	Musicians follow directions through playing from notations and learning instruments
3 **Analyse and solve problems** *Try to think logically*	Music involves solving technical as well as stylistic challenges
4 **Be accurate and punctual** *Employers don't like mistakes*	Music writing needs to be clear and precise; musicians work hard for excellence in performance at the advertised time
5 **Take decisions**	There are many opportunities in music for this (and negotiating with others)
6 **Value others' work** *Employers want good 'team players'*	Performing helps group co-operation and pleasure in joint achievement
7 **Communication** *Can you discuss well with others?*	You communicate through performing, composing and talking about music
8 **Show flexibility** *How amenable are you to thinking about alternative ways of doing something?*	Musicians are good at considering different methods of performance and interpretation

The study of music also stretches the imagination, builds confidence and develops a keen ear for sounds and language. Many people devote a great deal of their leisure time to music, and performing groups of all kinds provide an enviable base for meeting other young people with similar interests.

Music provision and grants

Local Education Authorities (LEAs)

In a state school classroom, music is statutory for ages 5–14 under National Curriculum entitlement (or recommended by Expressive Arts 5–14 in Scotland). Music education may include preparation for public examinations and is usually enriched by access to instrumental tuition. Recent changes in the way schools receive and spend money have meant that there is a wide variety of arrangements for bringing pupils into contact with instrumental or singing teachers. It is hoped that all pupils will have had access to this sort of training before taking decisions about their GCSE choices, and that, once embarked on a music course, free tuition will be available, as it normally is for practical aspects of other subjects.

Most LEAs have tried to maintain wide-ranging tuition and experience through local music centres, although this has not necessarily been free. In addition, bands, choirs, ensembles and orchestras which bring together the most advanced young musicians from a wide geographical (or large urban) area may have access to visiting tutors and conductors of national repute. They can include jazz, ethnic-music, big-band and recorder groups, and they often convene at weekends or during holidays, bringing together pupils from both state and independent sectors. Frequently, such musical groups can be excellent ambassadors through their fine performances abroad, just as schools are important in enriching the artistic life of the local community. Many perform in events such as the National Festival of Music for Youth and the Schools Proms.

Grants

Local government can award grants for higher education of many kinds, and if a course is 'designated' by the Department for Education and Employment (DfEE) it will attract a mandatory grant. This means that the LEA must provide the grant, subject to whatever deductions are made in respect of parental income. Other awards, for example for postgraduate courses, are 'discretionary', which means that the LEA is not obliged to offer them. If it does, it will almost certainly require musicians to audition. It may also be involved in grants for Music Theatre and Dance, some of which will be sought by 16- as well as 18-year-olds.

In all cases, you should approach the Post-school Awards section of your local LEA at latest by the end of the January before the start of the course, even if only on a fact-finding basis. They will not thank you for making first contact in May!

Some LEAs still offer support to young musicians who secure places in groups such as the National Youth Orchestras.

See also the sections on *Applications*, *Auditions* and *Performance* (**pages 24, 26 and 31**) in this book.

Choir, independent and specialist music schools

Choir schools

Over 40 choir schools offer music scholarships for promising young singers; these are usually part of preparatory, independent or voluntary aided schools. Recruitment has traditionally been of boys aged between seven and nine but, happily, girls' places are now more widely available. Arrangements may be in place to include participation by girls even though they may actually not be in a choir school. Training is also available for boys and girls from day schools, who are prepared to give time for choir practice, at major parish churches and some cathedrals.

Useful address

For further information, contact The Choir Schools' Association, The Minster School, Deangate, York YO1 2JA (telephone 01904 625217).

Independent schools

Overlapping the provision by choir schools are the music scholarships offered by 150 or so independent schools, which allow various percentages of fees to be waived. The present government's Assisted Places scheme applies in some of these schools. These arrangements are usually means-tested. Parents need to decide whether, despite the fees, the facilities in an independent school outweigh LEA provision.

Specialist music schools

In a different category are the specialist music schools, listed in this table.

School	Earliest entry age	Numbers
Wells Cathedral School, Somerset BA5 2ST (telephone 01749 672117)	8	c. 130 within 800
The Yehudi Menuhin School, Surrey KT11 3QQ (telephone 01932 864739)	9	c. 50
St Mary's School, Edinburgh EH3 7EB (telephone 0131 538 7766)	7	c. 50
Purcell School, Harrow, N. London HA1 3JS (telephone 0181 422 1284)	8	c. 150
Chetham's School of Music, Manchester M3 1SB (telephone 0161 834 9644)	7	c. 290

In these schools specialist musicians make up differing percentages of the total student intake. The Department for Education and Employment (DfEE) can subsidize fees for some pupils admitted to the four English schools, and has recently increased the total to 460. These are in addition to 170 at the Royal Ballet School and a small number at Arts Educational School, Tring, and Elmhirst Ballet School, Camberley. Fees are on a sliding scale according to parental income, but take into account the state funding. Enquiries about St Mary's should be made to the school.

Pimlico School, London SW1V 3AT (telephone 0171 828 0881) is a co-educational comprehensive school within Westminster City Council and has a small strongly musical intake within its 1300 students. There are also specialist arrangements at Douglas Academy, Glasgow and the Lothian Specialist Music School, Edinburgh.

Most of the above offer places for sixth-form entry, and the list of A-level successes, entries and scholarships into higher education is, not surprisingly, very impressive.

Options to discuss with parents and staff

Leaving school at 16?

The main options are:

- going on to further education or tertiary college or staying on to the sixth form
- taking an individual course, e.g. in office skills, or an apprenticeship
- finding employment, if it is available.

One useful way to find out what you want to do is to take up any work experience entitlement you may have. You can find out a great deal about the job at the actual work-place.

Some young people look for a job in retailing which keeps them close to music, at least in the recording field. Large groups such as Virgin or HMV in a major city might employ 40–50 people (some part-time) in their extensive CD and cassette sections. They also have more flexibility to engage relief staff and to organize proper training. Another store, such as Woolworth, with several non-music sections, might employ three people in the music section and take on more staff just for Saturdays. Knowledge of both the 'chart scene' and the classical repertoire will be valuable. This can be a first step. For further advice see *Sales* (**page 82**).

If you are continuing to study in the sixth form or at college, you will need to choose which courses to follow.

Public examinations and qualifications for the 16–19 age group are under review and new A-level and GNVQ courses will begin in 1998. There is a pilot scheme for a General National Vocational Qualification (GNVQ) in Performing Arts and Entertainment Industries being run in 150 centres. The first students to complete this course will be ready to seek higher education places in 1998.

Combinations of A and AS levels and GNVQs can be very important. Examination boards are moving towards inclusion of a stronger Music Technology element; ULEAC has moved furthest on this with a separate examination. Students with interests in Sound Recording will need to check whether, for example, Physics is required for entry to certain post-18 courses when making decisions about post-16 courses.

Moving on at 18?

The main options are:

- higher education (a degree-type course for three or four years)
- employment, if available
- taking a year out.

When you reach 18 more employment opportunities are available in music if you have A levels or GNVQs, whether or not these are in music. Again, training in office skills (perhaps including desk-top publishing) could prove useful. Other useful skills are:

- playing several instruments – demonstrating them in music shops
- foreign languages or physics – assisting in firms which have foreign or technical correspondence.

Employers value musicians' attributes highly, and have spoken about their abilities to understand the different requirements of customers in a shop. Therefore, if the employment and its contacts interest you, don't be too proud to start at the bottom of the organization, or too modest to think of a move after a suitable time.

The next section gives detailed information on some specific avenues available to you when you are 18 or over. Be careful to check the entry requirements and the status of any course that is not a full degree.

Decision-making at 18+

Researching higher education options in music

You need to sharpen the focus of your post-18 plans by – at the latest – Easter of your first year of sixth-form or FE college. The aspects you need to research are included in this chart.

Research topic	
Finding out more	Sources include: • schools, careers officers, instrumental and singing staff • LEA advisory service • older students already on courses (local youth music groups can provide valuable exchanges of this kind of information) • open days, where you can resolve queries on site.
Checking grades and grants	Assess A-level requirements, including practical grades, and whether your intended course qualifies for a mandatory grant. (Most university and conservatoire degree courses will.)
What about lessons?	If you are not going to a conservatoire, check whether the course provides free (or contributes to) instrumental or vocal tuition.

You should also ask yourself:

a) Do you want to specialize in music at 18+ but not have a career in it?

b) Is your keenness and determination to do music strong enough to withstand other people's doubts and setbacks on the way? If you are in doubt, take lots of advice and ensure that you're not being too modest!

The course should be chosen for what it offers *you* rather than, for example, because it has attracted a number of your friends. New and lasting relationships will spring from the new groups of colleagues elsewhere. As it will take up the most important three or four years of your life so far, it's the *course* which has to be right.

The *Music Education Yearbook* (details on **page ix**) is useful and can save you a great deal of time.

Universities, institutes and colleges of higher education

Please read this page with **pages 12–16**, as there is a good deal of common ground. There is some overlap in terminology between institutes of higher education (IHEs) and colleges of higher education (CHEs).

If you are seeking a place at a university or institute of higher education, you need to think about the following points.

- The tutorial system – is it individual (i.e. one-to-one) or seminar-based (i.e. group)?
- Is the course based on projects or modules (usually allowing wide choice) or is it mainly 'taught', i.e. by lectures?
- Is the assessment heavily weighted towards the final examination, or can you secure a substantial percentage through coursework?
- Is there a resident ensemble which gives tuition? Is there other tuition? Is tuition free?
- How strong is the research element within the department?
- How well resourced is the music technology element?
- How far is the department involved in music of non-western cultures or non-classical styles?
- Does the university – or do individual colleges – have choral or instrumental exhibitions?

Most of these queries can be answered 'yes' or 'no', while others can be resolved through instinct and strong impression. Admissions tutors will be interested to know why you choose their course, and you should be able to demonstrate both the thoroughness with which you've sifted the evidence and the factors which are important to you. Some answers may be found from older friends already at the institution.

You may also like to find out how entry to the university or college performing groups is organized.

Conservatoires normally recruit directly, but the City of Leeds College and the Welsh College of Music and Drama do so by means of UCAS.

These publications, in addition to those mentioned in the text, may be helpful:

- *Working in the Performing Arts*, COIC, £2.95 + 10% postage
- *Inside the Music Business*, Barrow and Newby, Blueprint, Chapman and Hall £15
- *Music* – a short 'questions and answers' book, Trotman, Richmond £3.50
- *The Musician's Handbook*, Rhinegold, £12.95 + £2 postage
- *Careers in Music*, a pamphlet published by ISM
- *How to set up a home recording studio*, Mellor, PC Publishing £8.95.

The abbreviations used above may be found in Appendix 3 with fuller details. Shorter articles appear in specialist journals and music education magazines such as the *Music Teacher*.

Case study: **Emma: Transferring from school to higher education**

Having gained grades B, B, C in my A levels (Music, English and French), I am now studying for a degree in Music with Education, and am thoroughly enjoying it. This is a modular course in which I do projects in both the Music and Education departments; this term I am currently involved in a Bach project; next term I will be studying 'Writing about childhood' in the Education department. I chose this course because I thought it would give me a broader perspective and increased job prospects, as opposed to a pure Music degree, and as I am interested in possibly combining a professional singing career with music therapy, I felt that the education part of the course would be useful in this area, although it does not give me Qualified Teacher Status.

The university is fantastic for music as there is so much to become involved in; I am in the Chamber choir, University choir, and am forming my own madrigal group. I am also in the symphony orchestra, and there also exists a chamber orchestra, Big Band, string quartets, and many more ensembles formed by students themselves. This is one of the greatest differences between sixth form and higher education; the ability to form small, successful ensembles, that perform at lunch-time concerts etc. Whereas at sixth-form level people would have joined existing ensembles, here, if they want to be part of a wind quintet or string quartet, they ask friends and form the group. Also, I am no longer studying three subjects as at A level, and have far more time to devote to practice.

Higher education attracts talented musicians from all areas of the country and abroad. From being well known as a singer at college, I am now just one of many singers, several bringing more talent and experience than myself. However, it is a stimulating learning process.

Moving to a new establishment invariably means a change in instrumental teachers and, after various consultations, I have been extremely fortunate in finding excellent teachers in both violin and voice. The MEDEA string quartet has just concluded a residency and I learned with the inspiring second violinist. My new singing teacher is also very helpful, and we are working mainly on technique at the moment.

Luckily, my own transfer from sixth form to higher education has been extremely smooth; my music is going from strength to strength with opportunities for music-making at a high level. My degree is academic; each project of seminars, lectures and performances is followed by a 5000-word essay, but since the choice of essay topic is more or less up to the individual, there is strong personal interest in the topic, and one can therefore write confidently.

I am currently having both harmony and keyboard harmony lessons which are entirely voluntary; I feel they are 'good' for me! This is mainly to keep up the harmony I learnt at A level which will always be useful.

My expectations have certainly been fulfilled, and I am thoroughly enjoying the challenges, both musical and otherwise, of Higher Education.

Teaching

If you want to teach music, try to plan your career path according to the commitment you might wish to make. Here are some questions, with possible avenues below. Do you want:

a) *To study music as a broad, academic discipline and later decide if you want to teach it?*
A university or college of higher education (CHE) non-teaching degree, followed immediately or later by a postgraduate Certificate in Education (PGCE) usually one year full-time, but the Open University now has an 18-month distance-learning PGCE.

b) *To have a performance bias for most of your degree and later decide if you want to teach?*
A conservatoire degree (mainly four-year) plus PGCE.

c) *To learn more about education alongside your music studies?*
A joint music and education course (hitherto B Ed and four years); new three-year BA/B Ed or BA/QTS courses are being established. QTS means Qualified Teacher Status.
NB not all 'Music and Education' courses give QTS.

Some Music degrees (and joint-Arts or joint-subject degrees) have modular arrangements. This means that you can accumulate credits as the course progresses, rather than having nearly all the assessment dependent on final examinations. All could be followed by a PGCE. Teaching music at secondary school or further education level requires a substantial subject specialization at degree level.

Special notes

1 For mature students (21+) some two-year B Ed secondary training courses, building on other music qualifications, are available.

2 All entrants to teacher training courses require GCSE Maths and English (or their equivalents) at Grade C or above. For those born on or after 1 September 1979, starting primary teacher training courses from September 1998, GCSE Science at Grade C or above will also be required. High-level practical skills in music may need to be demonstrated.

3 Teacher training institutions work in partnership with schools and most of your time (e.g. 24 of 36 weeks on a PGCE course) will be spent in school supported by a mentor or professional tutor.

4 Currently, there is a salary incentive for a high final classification in 'honours' degrees.

5 During your main training, think about whether where you might want to work might influence your choice of course, e.g.
   – an independent school (where QTS may not be required)
   – a Local Education Authority maintained school
   – a grant-maintained or 'opted-out' school
   – a school with a religious foundation
   – a further education college.

6 You may wish to teach instrumental or vocal studies in schools, or privately. For further information see the relevant sections in Part 2.

Conservatoires

Much imaginative rethinking of conservatoire courses has taken place recently, providing both a broader view of training in performance and a realistic view of how the graduate so equipped can operate in the changing professional world.

Potential conservatoire students will often be able to gauge standards through contact with local successful entrants, as well as through the advice of experienced teachers. The ratio of applications to acceptances varies from perhaps 5 : 1 to 13–14 : 1 (with tuba and harp in the former category). This means that, for example, a large vocal department could have as many as 250–300 applications for 20 or 30 places.

A very high percentage of the members of the excellent orchestras, smaller instrumental and vocal ensembles and soloists who enrich our professional musical life are ex-students of the conservatoires, and there is no doubt that the rigorous training at these is the background to a successful career in performance. Although titles and status of courses change slightly from time to time, those in the nine main conservatoires of the UK are now largely degree-based. The graduate courses will:

a)   attract students for whom performance elements have been and will continue to be strong
b)   be demanding in terms of time because of the challenging range of studies to be pursued.

A performance-biased course (or degree plus postgraduate performance) is likely to be the main choice for the singer or player thought to have a chance of success in that fiercely competitive area. Remember that many more students with a determined performance interest are trained than can be accommodated in those parts of the performing profession that can provide a reasonable livelihood. Entrance to a performance course with the thought, 'Oh well, if it doesn't work I can always teach,' is not a good baseline, if no teacher-training is also in view. Most musicians teach at some stage in their careers, and it is hoped that some formal training is undertaken. The attributes needed by a good teacher are outlined on **pages 46–49.**

Although conservatoires are not the only institutions in which conductors and composers can develop their talents, they will inevitably offer distinguished tutoring in those departments. The very existence of a large student body in a conservatoire provides scope for the composer or conductor. Both will be interested in the quality of the resources for sound recording and music technology.

Several conservatoires have developed strands such as Communication and Teaching Skills and Study and Vocational Options, and these demonstrate the flexibility of thinking about students' needs. Some elements concentrate on studies which support all aspects of performance, while others make students aware of likely employment opportunities in the wider world of 'the music business'. Conservatoires have been reviewing arrangements for being intermediaries for jobs while students are still in training. Staff strike a delicate balance between the requirements of coursework and assisting students to gain a foothold in the professional circuit.

Most institutions will readily answer queries prior to final application – informally, or perhaps at an 'advisory audition'; such an enquiry will not prejudice your chances at a later stage. You should check with each college separately whether this facility is offered. Another factor is access to a particular teacher with whom you may already have worked. Think about whether that really is the most important consideration.

You may want to consider having a year off before your main training. If a college has accepted you – and is content to leave your place open for a year – there is little problem, except that it would be wise to ask your parents if they will support you in the intervening period. If you simply feel that you need another year to prepare yourself for entry, remember that further maturity and technical skill will be expected from the extra year's work when you audition or re-apply!

Other higher education

Although discussed in some detail, universities and conservatoires may not be the first choice for musicians at 18+. Colleges and institutes of higher education offer an impressive variety of courses which bring together students engaged in different disciplines. They often have broad study options, and each may offer both teacher-training and music degrees at undergraduate level; entry criteria can be demanding. Some have strong postgraduate musician contingents and this mixture of disciplines and career-intentions (often with very good residential accommodation) attracts many students.

Degree-level courses in Musical Instrument Technology may also be available.

Some practical points

In the summer of each year, higher education institutions publish information about entry in the autumn of the next calendar year, so be prepared for the sequence to last 15 months.

If you don't secure the required grades, keep calm, talk to your own school or college and be prepared for a long stint on the telephone. Make sure that you understand the procedures for 'clearing' if you wish to take that option. The broadsheet national newspapers publish very helpful information in the days after A-level and equivalent results are known, as does CEEFAX.

Although conservatoires, universities and colleges of higher education have many common factors in what they offer, be clear about your choice of type of course and write your application convincingly. Ask a parent or teacher to check a draft first. There is further advice on making applications on **pages 23–4**.

Remember that it's *your* career, not anybody else's.

Useful publications, together with the *Music Education Yearbook*, which should be available in school include:

- *Degree Course Offers* (Heap) – Trotman, 12 Hill Rise, Richmond, Surrey TW10 6UA (priced at about £16)
- *CRAC Degree Course Guide (Music with Drama and Dance)* – Hobson Publishing, Bateman Street, Cambridge CB2 1LZ (priced at about £5)
- *Which Subject, Which Career?*, Consumers' Association/Hobsons, 2 Marylebone Rd, London, NW1 4DF
- ECCTIS – a government-owned computerized information service covering 80,000 courses in higher education. Facilities should be available through careers staff.

Career pathways at 18+

Here are the main pathways and possible avenues of study through the 18–22 age period. The path through the columns may be diagonal not horizontal.

Broad category of pathway at 18+	Degree course type	Some postgraduate courses or area of teaching
Teaching	B Ed or BA/B Sc/QTS	Primary, Secondary, Adults Instrumental, Vocal, private (PGCE after non-teaching degree)
Academic bias	University, music or joint, or non-music*	PGCE, or PG performance, composition, Advanced specialist MA/M Mus Music Therapy
Performance bias	Probably conservatoire but possibly: World Musics Band Musicianship Jazz Options Performing Arts	Most PGCE as other postgraduate performance
Music and Science/ Technology Recording/Instrument maintenance	e.g. B Mus 'Tonmeister'** Joint physics/instrumental music*** Music and recording	Most PG courses as other
Year out	Abroad Temporary employment Further practice Retakes	As other
Straight to employment	Possibly in a post close to performance, or the music industry	See Appendix 1: Jobs in Music advertised in 1996 (**page 100**) and *Sales* (**pages 82–3**).

NB   *   No bar to PG Music access after non-music degree, but check grant position.
   **   Surrey University
   ***   For example Imperial College/Royal College of Music four-year B.Sc. in Physics and Studies in Music Performance

The postgraduate and research sectors offer a limited number of places in departments through which masters' degrees and doctorates may be worked for.

Destinations of graduates

The UK higher education system has the capacity to produce over 2000 music graduates each year. That includes the conservatoires (about 750) and the Music Technology courses, but not the Open University, teacher training graduates or figures for students not completing courses. Reliable statistics for destinations of graduates are not readily available on a national basis, particularly in the performance sector, but it will always be reasonable for you to ask for information about where the graduates who have left your intended course have gone.

The line between the freelance professional and the 'musician who earns some money as a performer' is unclear, but musicians basically have a wider choice than many in the various avenues of occasional, seasonal or combinations of part-time work. They can work at any time of day, and half the night. For a survey on work within two or three years of leaving training, many would report performing/teaching, some would log modest income from writing/broadcasting and the fortunate very few might enter 'lecturing on cruise liners'. If posts *are* secured quickly after graduation it is more likely that classroom teachers and music technology graduates will find full-time posts than some of their colleagues.

The pages on *Performing* (**page 31**), *Combining teaching and performing* (**page 50**) and *Posts not advertised* (**page 28**) may give further ideas. Arts graduates are said to 'like working with people' and this may counter a claim from employers that graduates often lack inter-personal skills.

A survey by York University over a recent five-year period showed a fairly even split between Employment Gained and Further Study.

In **Employment Gained**:

Music posts in Creative/Media accounted for a third (including cathedral bass, répétiteur, journalist, music copyist). The next main group was a particularly interesting 'miscellaneous' including high-level administration and retail, together with commissioned officer (RAF) and accountancy.

In the **Further Study Group**:

There were roughly equal proportions between advanced performance, teacher training and higher degrees. However, national statistics often show nearly 50 per cent of the *Further Study in Music* group going into teacher training. Patterns do, however, shift.

York's Music Technology B Sc graduates naturally show a different profile, with software-hardware, sound engineering and similar development posts predominating, but with 'freelance musician' also listed. Surrey's 'Tonmeister' course alumni will show similar destination statistics but also have a wide spread.

A summary of conservatoire graduates pursuing further study will show up to 90 per cent pursuing advanced performance studies, with very few moving to formal teacher training as such. Higher education institutes will show yet another complexion, reflecting some interesting study options in latter stages.

Musicians are no different from other graduates – nearly all seek a job, further training or a rich benefactor. Interestingly, up to five per cent of music graduates go on to a career in finance.

Ask for information about where the graduates from your course go and what help the careers service will give you.

Two general quotes which appeared in the original edition of this book are still relevant, and not just for graduates:

- *Think if the way you see yourself is the way an employer would wish to see you.* (from a MORI survey)
- *Finding a job is not a single event, but a process ... towards both decision-making and a revision of attitudes ... with the development of skills in self-presentation. This takes time and there are no short cuts.* (Sheffield University Careers Advisory Service)

Research suggests that it is slightly harder to obtain a place on a music degree course than the national subject average. It is encouraging that the Higher Education Funding Council for England (HEFCE) report well of the next milestone. Having assessed for quality 53 music departments in universities, colleges of higher education and four conservatoires, they stated:

Music graduates have a good employment record. The majority, in some cases as many as 95 per cent of a graduating cohort, secure employment or enrol for postgraduate study within six months of grad-uation. Of these, some enter the music profession as performers, com-posers, journalists, advisers, managers, technicians or teachers; many are freelance and self-employed. Others find employment elsewhere. As a result of their highly-developed collaborative and transferable skills, music graduates are becoming increasingly attractive to employers in industry, retailing and other areas.

(Source: *Subject overview report: Music,* Higher Education Funding Council for England, p. 12)

Postgraduate courses

Performance and composition

Most conservatoires offer postgraduate performance/advanced study courses. Applicants will come from conservatoires themselves (sometimes involving a change of institution), universities and other HE colleges. Specialities might be Jazz/Rock, Early Music, Composition (including for screen), Conducting, Accompanying and Electronic Techniques, but you will not always find all these in one place.

Currently, the Guildhall School of Music and Drama is the only source of a postgraduate diploma in Orchestral Studies. The National Opera Studio – see below – takes singers some time after their main training. It also trains répétiteurs, whose accompanying skills lie mainly in the operatic repertoire and who coach singers in musical – and often language – aspects of their roles.

Local Authority awards are hard to come by in this postgraduate area – **see page 5.** Note also that these courses are different from the postgraduate academic provision in both university and conservatoire sectors, which are usually called 'higher degrees'.

National Opera Studio

This is a one-year course in London and is organized as follows.

Status of entrants	• Singing students post main training, usually with at least two years' experience after college. Average age: 27 • Experienced répétiteurs
Numbers taken each year	• 12 singers (not necessarily spread over the four main voices) and three répétiteurs
Aims	• To apply the trained voice to the specifics of opera, e.g. stagecraft, languages, characterization, working with producers and conductors, and at least annually an opera house orchestra. The Studio can help both those who already have some engagements with companies, and singers who wish to take on brief engagements during the course. • To give experience to répétiteurs in coaching singers in a variety of roles, and in direction of rehearsals.

Enquiries to

National Opera Studio c/o Morley College, 61 Westminster Bridge Road, Lambeth North, London SE1 7HT (telephone 0171 928 6833).

Postgraduate Certificate Of Education (PGCE)

Forty institutions in Great Britain and Northern Ireland offer PGCE courses in Music, normally of one year duration, full-time. Those considered most attractive fill their places very quickly in the autumn term prior to entry.

Useful addresses

Applications for England and Wales should be sent to:

- *The Graduate Teacher Training Registry (GTTR)*, Fulton House, Jessop Avenue, Cheltenham, Gloucestershire GL50 3SH (telephone 01242 225868)

Procedures are different in Northern Ireland and Scotland. Some useful addresses are:

- *The Department of Education for Northern Ireland*, Rathgael House, Balloo Road Bangor, Co. Down BT19 2PR (telephone 01247 279279)
- *The Advisory Service on Entry to Teaching*, c/o GTC, 5 Royal Terrace, Edinburgh EH7 5AF (telephone 0131 556 0072).

See also the section on *Teaching* (**pages 13 and 46–50**).

At the time of publication, it appears that there may be a shortage of qualified music teachers in the late 1990s. The profession needs to attract the best young musicians; it is hoped that they will wish to spend some time learning how to be good teachers.

The following places have a tradition of making additional arrangements for intending instrumental teachers within the PGCE in Music: Bath College of HE, Bretton Hall University College, University of Central England in Birmingham and Middlesex University.

Recent developments include part-time distance-learning courses offered by the Open University, among others. The OU course starts in February and lasts 18 months, and you have to nominate a school which has agreed to act as a base for your major school experience. You do not go through GTTR for entry. The telephone number of the OU PGCE Central Office is 01908 652996/653016; they publish a brochure. There is also a school-centred initial teacher training arrangement (SCITT) where a consortium of schools, rather than a college, supervises the training package.

The Royal Northern College of Music (RNCM) now links with Manchester Metropolitan University (MMU) for a two-year Secondary PGCE. RNCM's well-established Junior Strings project is dove-tailed with the university's long-standing teacher training and schools contacts. Full coverage of National Curriculum work is offered with continuance of students' own lessons and a strong context of Dalcroze and Kodàly work. The course attracts a mandatory grant.

Newer developments and courses

Some interesting examples showing the diversity of higher education courses are given below. At the time this book is published, some will not have taken their first cohort through. The list is offered for information, and will need to be seen in the context of the many other, long-established, courses.

Huddersfield University, now offers a BA for Music with English, or with Modern Languages, or with Theatre Studies.

The Royal Scottish Academy of Music and Drama (RSAMD, telephone 0141 332 4101) offers a BA in Scottish Music.

Liverpool Institute of the Performing Arts (LIPA, telephone 0151 707 0002) is a new HE development concentrating on the entertainment and cultural industries, and seeking to train versatile designers, performers and managers. There are six routes, including Music, to the three-year honours degree, and a Dip HE in Sound Technology.

The Musicians' Institute in East London (telephone 0171 265 0284) has developed a number of courses at several levels and styles in the popular music area. The one-year diploma covers a wide variety of performance aspects via projects, tutorials and workshops.

The Guitar Institute Guitar School (telephone 0181 740 1031) offers a Dip HE in Popular Music Performance.

Kingston University (telephone 0181 547 7149) offers a postgraduate MA Music for teachers, composers and performers. It takes one year full-time or two years part-time (evenings), is modular and contains a strong research element in its second phase.

Trinity College of Music (telephone 0171 935 5773) has recently established a four-year B Music (TCM) which delivers Study Options as well as Vocational Options in the final year. The latter relate aspects of the music profession to today's employment market and include Publishing, Management, Teaching and Music Therapy. There is also a new MA in Music Education designed to bring together both performers and teachers.

West Lothian College, Scotland (telephone 01506 634300) has an HNC in Business Administration, Copyright Law and setting up recording companies.

Napier University, Edinburgh (telephone 0131 455 4330) offers a two-year HND in Music Studies.

There is a modular BA in World Musics at *King Alfred's College,* Winchester, a BA in Commercial Music at the *University of Westminster,* and a BA in Popular Music Studies at *Bretton Hall*.

Buckinghamshire College has recently established a BA in Music Industry Management which covers administration and marketing across many areas of music as well as law, finance and media.

Keele University has a new postgraduate MSc in Music Psychology, and York a part-time MA in Community Music.

Roehampton Institute, London, has an MA in Choral Education.

Rose Bruford College (telephone 0181 300 3024), well renowned for training and education in Theatre Arts, now offers a BA in Actor-musician and in Music Technology. There is also a distance-learning degree (one which does not require residence) in Opera. These examples may interest students whose skills are evenly balanced between theatre and music.

Each institution will have several more courses on offer.

A new National Centre for Popular Music is proposed, to be based in Sheffield.

Applying for jobs

Where to look for jobs

Jobs in and around the musical world are found in particular places. For most straightforward teaching posts you would look in the *Times Educational Supplement* on Fridays and the *Guardian* on Tuesdays. On Saturdays and Mondays in its 'Creative and Media' section, the *Guardian* has a selection of some posts directly in music, but also some where there is a strong musical element. *Classical Music*, fortnightly, and the *Daily Telegraph* on Saturdays have a selection of music vacancies, as does *The Stage* for posts where the theatre element predominates.

Some advice

Please remember that someone has to be attracted by your application so don't give them any reason for discarding it.

- Write on larger – rather than smaller – paper, and do a draft first.
- If you have to give the information on a form, read it through, to plan where you will state various things.
- Know what 'curriculum vitae' (CV) means – strictly speaking, 'the course of life', practically, information about your education, examinations, degrees, certificates, other interests and awards.
- Type or word-process the CV if possible, and save it onto a disk so that you can amend it later.
- Don't assume that what you consider your work strengths are all that the interviewers want to challenge you on; it may be important for them that your 'personality' fits in with existing staff.
- Note whether a letter of application is required, with or without CV. Such a letter should say why you want the post or place.
- If you have to fill in an application form, make sure that all relevant information is given. The reader may not be entranced by long lists of your early swimming certificates or dancing grades, but may be interested in a higher level Duke of Edinburgh award.
- If a photo is required, try to send a better-than-basic one.
- Make sure that someone else casts an eye over your papers before you send them.

Elementary errors

These include:

- omitting essential information, such as your telephone number or imminent change of address
- disregarding requests for information to be set out in a particular way, or for testimonials

- not making clear on the envelope for whom the application is intended
- forgetting to give referees' names and addresses
- neglecting to show interest e.g. by finding out one or two things about the firm or institution being applied to
- sending messy photocopies, cassettes or videos
- missing the closing date.

After training

At a later stage when some professional work is coming in, a decision may need to be made about references etc. It may then be more sensible to use current section leaders rather than the referees who supported you earlier but are not working in your current field. 'Fixers' who have a considerable influence in offering work on the margins of top groups, and indeed some complete ensembles, need to know that musicians they hire can adapt immediately to all circumstances. They tend to stick with those whose quality of work and reliability they know. Much work is passed by word of mouth.

See also *Auditions* (**pages 26–27**) and *Performance* (**pages 31–8**).

The Value of Music (National Music Council/University of Westminster) gives further detail in support of music's claim to be an extensive employer – for example the recording industry directly employs 11,000 people, and music education and training half as many again. A fascinating picture is provided of consumer attendances and purchases, public expenditure, promotion and many other aspects of the 'music business'.

Auditions

What do auditions involve?

Auditions are different from grade examinations. They tend to be related to a competition itself, or for places, perhaps in an orchestra or for a higher education course, rather than an examination test against a standard marking system. You might need to talk more about your music-making, or play fewer scales!

At any level of audition, good preparation is essential. Check, from information supplied or your own enquiries, the required length of performance and tests to be expected (including whether you will be required to improvise). Will an accompanist be provided free? If you are offering percussion, organ or anything requiring music technology it is wise to make sure what is on hand. These questions may also arise:

- Will demonstration on more than one instrument be required?
- May singers be asked to sight-read from a *choral* score?
- How will conductors and composers be assessed – will there be a group to conduct or a requirement to submit cassettes of works? Would the composer and colleagues be allowed to perform, say, a recent composition for trio or quartet?

Some advice

- Make sure prescribed pieces are easily available and that there is no difficulty over particular editions, or a copy for your accompanist.
- Arrive early and warm up, and err on the side of dressing smartly but comfortably.
- You may take a photocopy of a page to assist you or your accompanist with a difficult turn-over, and a copy for the panel, provided that the original material is in use at the time and the photocopies are destroyed afterwards.
- Be prepared to announce your music clearly, and with reasonable pronunciation of foreign titles.
- If you are taking in two instruments, find out for which of them sight-reading may be required. You may have the choice, in which case arrange the sequence of instruments sensibly.
- If you are asked to provide an accompanist, do so without fail, even at your own expense.
- It is particularly important that post-training students applying for discretionary awards from LEAs, trusts or scholarships should realize that expectations – not only in terms of performance but also presentation and the sense of 'meaning business' – are much greater than at 18+. Panels will not be sympathetic to lateness, forgotten music, ill-rehearsed accompaniments, scruffy dress, off-hand communication with the organizing office or inability to talk enthusiastically about musical experiences gained and hoped for.

Show realism with ambition in your answers, and show evidence that you have already taken steps to advance your career.

At this stage it is also sensible to make practical enquiries such as:

- In a postgraduate course, how much tuition will you receive, are there ensemble/vocal group classes, what orchestra/choir opportunities will definitely be offered, and will these need to be auditioned for?
- For a trust award, are there particular obligations to report at the end of the course undertaken, is the money paid directly, are there restrictions on how it is spent and, for courses abroad, are travel costs claimable?

Posts not advertised

There is a small section of employment which could be called 'Jobs that aren't applied for'. Here is a list of examples of such jobs.

- A performance group establishes itself locally and in its training institution, and gradually finds paid employment in its specialist sphere.
- Friends combine in an unusual ensemble (for example, the London Serpent Trio) and offer themselves as an alternative attraction.
- A graduate, having taken full advantage of generous facilities at college, makes headway by building a clientele there and on a wider basis afterwards. Recording techniques and video-making suggest themselves.
- Another student combines a music qualification with a business studies course, and builds a practice in a particular area of accountancy, with music and arts performers as target group.
- An instrument technology diploma-holder takes baroque instruments as a main interest and gradually establishes expertise in valuing stringed instruments for music shops and auction houses.
- A young part-time teacher in a rural area is frequently being asked to advise on and seek the purchase of instruments and music and gradually sees that the 'business' can expand into a more formal retailing arrangement. (**NB** There are some dangers of conflicting interest in the interim.)
- A qualified musician decides to chance financial existence on combinations of private teaching, reviewing books and local concerts, being a church organist, accompanying a choir, composing, music copying for a publisher and teaching the clarinet at a music centre.

Few of the posts listed above, with the exception of parts of the last example, will be advertised. Success will have come through determination, use of initiative, attractive presentation of the service or services you are offering, and the ability to take risks and remain optimistic in the early stages.

These avenues may be explored at any time in a career, not only at the outset.

2

Careers in Music

Instrumental performance

The job

Work in this area involves playing:

- in large groups such as bands and orchestras
- in smaller ensembles specializing in jazz, popular music in all its variety, folk and chamber music groups or
- as a soloist.

All these occupations may entail unsociable hours, extensive travel and an entirely freelance career, and for any combination of them you will need a flexible attitude to a variety of musical styles and practices.

Skills and abilities required

The player of any instrument needs dedication, stamina, technical expertise of a high order, the ability to make musical responses and enthusiasm for the life-style. Soloists have to memorize a great many works but can make decisions about some aspects of the performance; most other players, while being generally free from the pressure of singular exposure, have to tailor their performances to the demands of different music directors.

If the group is small, individual members can make suggestions about the presentation of the performance, and be involved in the development of style. This will be as important in an Early Music group as a jazz combination specializing in a particular mode. For better or worse, competitions have a high profile in the music world; almost inevitably a young player will undergo this experience either in public or in an audition for a group or orchestra. For brass bands, it is a regular feature.

Playing venues differ. A cathedral organist will operate in very different surroundings from those of military bands playing at the FA Cup Final and all instrumentalists must be able to deal equally with changes of environment and working colleagues. Nowadays, communication as well as practical skills are being sought from many young musicians. Some additional attributes may be demanded of, for example, keyboard players. Most organists will need to be in sympathy with denominational rituals; accompanists and coaches will need to develop added strengths such as familiarity with a wide repertoire from all categories; keyboard/synthesizer players ought to master the possibilities opened up by advances in music technology.

Opportunities

Practicalities dictate opportunities – there are more full-time posts for violinists than harpists. In another sense, a trumpeter can find work in more kinds of music-making than can a player of the cor anglais. Openings will vary geographically, but all groups have to attract and retain audiences through the excellence of both their performance and presentation/publicity. It is possible for a few musicians to spend a high proportion of their time playing in a specialized area, for example contemporary orchestral works or original baroque instruments. However, most players will need to adapt to make the most of freelance opportunities: they could find themselves recording a TV jingle in the morning and playing a Brahms symphony in the evening. The 'pop' scene is almost a law unto itself, with new groups rising to fame with invigorating frequency. Some of them attract extremely lucrative contracts.

Instrumentalists involved in professional performances belong to the Musicians' Union, and may also be members of the Incorporated Society of Musicians.

Training

Formal post-school training will most likely be at a conservatoire, unless a decision has been made to take a more academic degree before specializing in performance. You should check whether two A levels are still required as a minimum to secure a mandatory award for a conservatoire course. Professional training is also available through the armed services' Schools of Music. (Please see *Playing opportunities in the Armed Services,* **page 45**, and *Postgraduate courses: Performance and composition*, **page 20**). Do not assume that formal training on an unusual instrument is not available – ask! Even within traditional areas queries should be raised. For example, a keyboard player might wish to know whether specialities such as accompaniment, harpsichord or opera coaching are catered for on the course.

Young players of whatever style of music have to work hard to get launched, and should take advantage of any training opportunity, formal or otherwise, short or extensive, to further their mastery and enjoyment of the instrument. Young jazz devotees who probably make their initial contacts through local clubs or music centres might explore the B Music with Jazz option available at some conservatoires, or other courses which offer it as a module. The City of Leeds College has a full-time Jazz Studies course and the University of Salford has several courses in Popular Music, Recording and Band Musicianship. (For the 16–19 age-group, Perth in Scotland offers an HND in Rock Music, and other colleges of further education a BTEC in Popular Music.)

In another area, developing a repertoire in chamber groups might give access to high-level coaching not available to the members in other circumstances.

Rarely, in the classical field, some individuals and groups achieve success without the disciplines of formal music training. However, deliberately bypassing that, while aspiring to solid employment may mean giving up experiences that could develop wide-ranging musicianship, and missing out on contacts who will be helpful later. In a profession which is clearly seeking greater flexibility of approach and attributes, broadening your performance experience at a high level and taking part in Communication

Skills courses such that as at Guildhall School of Music and Drama (incidentally the only conservatoire currently offering a postgraduate course in orchestral training) will always be advantageous.

There are very few full-time jobs in solo instrumental performance, and not all orchestras employ players on a solid contractual, salaried basis. Skills in personal and organizational affairs such as tax, expenses claims, reliable modes of travel etc., will be at a premium for those involved in freelance – i.e. not salaried – work. Careful attention to diary planning (particularly if you are teaching as well) will be vital. You might ask whether these very practical points are dealt with on your course. You could also find out whether varied performance opportunities will be managed by the college administration, to provide a number of 'mini-platforms' for advanced students before they venture into the professional world.

Professional orchestras

Many aspiring orchestral players will have started thinking about a professional career while in senior positions in the excellent LEA youth orchestras. Progression may be via the demands and excitements of, for example, National Youth Orchestra, and 'pre-professional' groups such as the Young Musicians' Symphony Orchestra, the London Philharmonic Youth Orchestra or Camerata Scotland.

Procedures for recruitment vary but broadly the main orchestras will:

- advertise posts and receive 30–80 applications for each one
- consider applications straight from conservatoires
- audition a good proportion of those who apply, on standard repertoire as well as sight-reading
- offer post-audition trials to a handful – these trials may last for months, possibly inconclusively
- expect successful applicants to be amenable personalities as well as first-class players and musicians.

Some orchestras will audition for the 'deputy list'; some will prefer postgraduate experience. As will be seen from the ratio of applicants to posts, jobs are hard to come by. Even if you apply for nearly every job you see, you should be clear in your mind why you want to join a particular orchestra. If you applied to the Welsh National Opera Orchestra or Northern Sinfonia you would presumably substantiate the attractions to you of a mainly operatic or a mainly small orchestra repertoire respectively. This is in addition to geographical considerations.

Student training schemes are available in areas close to some major orchestras. A number are developing in association with particular conservatoires, or a wider range of HE institutions. The English Northern Philharmonia (the orchestra of Opera North) has co-operated with HE institutions for many years, and has ten players in for fifteen days over a twelve-month period. The scheme, which involves seven colleges and universities, is supported by the Musicians' Union. In a separate scheme, the orchestra has extended the liaison to composers aged up to 30. Other arrangements vary but most follow the principle that young orchestral players learn most quickly by joining existing practitioners and experiencing the standards and commitment required.

Clearly, the 'extra' or deputy work is usually the first step into the orchestral scene, and this is where the audition 'round' will start, bringing useful experience. Sometimes taking an initial post abroad is helpful.

The last decade has seen many changes in the way professional orchestras work and flourish. Most have needed to review both finances, including the flexibility of some players' contracts, and strategies for attracting and retaining audiences. Some have been awarded 'residences' or established more satisfactory permanent rehearsal arrangements. Less happily, the debate about how many major orchestras even capital cities can sustain – or recording companies keep on long contracts – continues.

All this has a bearing on recruitment, as do the welcome developments of outreach work to schools, hospitals and other communities mentioned elsewhere. A well-skilled and versatile young player potentially has a wider field of professional activity than was the case a generation ago, even though some of the more traditional areas of freelancing are diminishing. If string quartets continue to appear backing the main artist on the Lottery show, who knows what may ensue?

See *Auditions* (**pages 26–27**) and *Applying for jobs* (**pages 24–25**).

Case study: **Amanda**

Amanda, a freelance bassoonist, now well established in the profession, recalls a mixture of ill-paid but interesting playing opportunities initially with student colleagues in the year or so after training. She also worked in the underwear department of a famous store, in difficult early days. A short-term contract with a ballet company led to important and lasting contacts being made. She maintains that the sometimes routine nature of her work even now, is made very worthwhile by the occasional stunning concert where the audience is wildly enthusiastic. Her views on some conductors are not repeatable, and she suggests that orchestras and choirs often seem to know works better than those directing them.

Amanda stresses the positive nature of work by orchestras in developing educational projects, as long as all parties involved do the necessary preparation.

Singing

The job

This area of work involves singing:

- as a soloist in any branch of vocal music, with or without accompaniment or microphone
- as a member of a versatile professional choir or stage chorus
- in a cathedral, synagogue or other denominational context.

Skills and abilities required

Most of the text on instrumental performance also applies to singing, so please refer to that section (**pages 31–34**) as well.

It is important that school students seek out a helpful teacher and a good standard of performance experience in a group – at school or through a local choir – which has good vocal coaching. Knowing your natural range, and how to use your voice sensibly, will also allow you to cross over into folk and popular styles and develop a repertoire. Boys' voices will change in their early teens; mature voices can also change their character. Broadening your knowledge of music and maintaining skills (particularly facility with the keyboard) is also strongly advised.

Audition panels like a voice to be clean and clear, but with some colour and individuality. They like to hear musical expressiveness in the vocal line and an awareness of how that line is communicating to the listener.

In the profession, versatility and good musicianship are highly prized. Accurate sight-reading and a strong sense of pitch are vital attributes; not all contemporary choral scores are notated in traditional form. Very few singers are salaried: the busy freelancer may be part of a backing group for a TV recording in the morning and a soloist in *Messiah* in the evening. This adaptability will be a huge asset until the career can have a sharper focus. (Alongside this, it's fair to point out that a voice which blends well in a madrigal group may not always translate easily to high-profile solos in the latest London rock musical, or one that is suitable for operetta to the reflective solos in an oratorio.)

Authentic pronunciation, often requiring individual tuition, of both modern languages and Latin may be called for in any branch of singing. To these attributes acting skills must be added for music-theatre (the name generally covering stage shows and musicals) and opera. In these two areas much time is taken on essential but non-musical aspects such as stage rehearsals, make-up and costume. The early rehearsals for an opera often take place months before the first performance.

Opportunities

Often, participation in a stage work or thrilling engagement in a joint choirs event will stimulate you to further involvement. The good singer whose voice is well cared-for will not lack opportunities for many years after school – this applies as much to those in choral societies as to lead singers in bands in pubs and clubs. Find an enthusiastic accompanist who enjoys exploring a wide repertoire.

The very few singers who can earn a complete living as soloists can afford to specialize. Many others seek a regular income from contract work in the major opera houses (usually starting in the chorus) or from seasonal engagements with touring groups. The BBC has traditionally limited its contract work to the BBC Singers. They have a six-month trial period which may then become a three-year contract, renewable for one year, one year in advance. They may offer a series of engagements with other productions, and try to be flexible if the singer secures solo work. Elsewhere, employment is on a freelance and sessional basis, often involving extensive travel but with jobs increasing through recommendation and good luck, in a mixture of solo and chorus work.

Other involvement may include being a vocalist in, for example, a barber-shop quartet or a member of a gospel choir. (Many of the latter have church affiliations. One, the London Adventist Chorale, won the adult section of Sainsbury's Choir of the Year in 1994.) The enjoyable choral activities mentioned on this page rarely produce a substantial income for the individual singers, although their training staff, conductors and accompanists may well be employed on a professional basis by the organization.

Training

Please see *Choir schools* (**page 6**) and similar training. Whether or not that early route or private tuition has been taken, the next main avenues of full-time study are:

- conservatoire (as first or second study)
- university (possibly as a choral scholar – male or female – but this may not provide individual tuition)
- college of higher education (as a prominent performance element)
- college or school concentrating on training for music-theatre.

The voice usually settles later than the normal training period and conservatoires would ideally have singing students in their twenties. The choices seem to be either finding employment in the interim, or concentrating on singing only after a different full-time course. Do not let your other music studies lapse.

It is very important to keep in contact with your LEA Awards section. Few offer postgraduate awards and they tend not to favour changes of subject. This can be frustrating for potential singers who graduate in modern languages, a seemingly very sensible combination.

Operatic performances will be hard to come by during school days, but you may already have developed a promising stage presence in other dramatico-musical events or been inspired by performances by national youth groups. Please note that the training for *music-theatre* usually takes place between the ages of about 16 and 19. LEA awards may be available for this, subject to audition. Also:

- some conservatoires limit their Opera School to third- and fourth-year students – the Royal Academy of Music and Royal College of Music have a joint Vocal Studies Faculty
- the National Opera Studio is for postgraduates.

See also *The performing arts* (**pages 38–39**).

Case study: **Simon**

Simon, a younger colleague in the singing profession first 'got the bug' through selection for the National Youth Choir. He gained a Choral Exhibition at university, although reading Modern Languages, and is grateful to have absorbed such a wealth of choral tradition (very useful later on) through singing in chapel, as well as seeking solo engagements. He also reports having a hard time initially and needed to do a PGCE and take a Languages teaching post to finance a year's singing tuition at the Royal Northern College of Music. There was a chance to join one of the cathedral choirs but good fortune brought him a series of deputy jobs and short opera seasons. He maintains that it's important to think hard about what music to sing at auditions, and to continue to have lessons, particularly when on the audition circuit and performing various styles.

The performing arts

Alongside the development of Expressive/Creative/Performing Arts work at GCSE, A level and for GNVQ and BTEC, there has been an increase in such courses in higher education. These offer a wider view of the performance arts and their possible integration, and those of degree status normally attract mandatory grants.

The job

You could be working in performance areas where two or more disciplines interact. Examples are music-theatre, 'shows', cabaret and revues. (Opera also fits this description but is usually considered separately.)

Skills and abilities required

A combination of convincing artistic expression and considerable physical resilience is necessary. In performance, swift changes from acting to dance, to chorus or solo singing will be commonplace, and all will involve a variety of styles from one show to another as well as possibly hundreds of performances of the same character. You will need to be clear about your intentions at an early stage. Aspiring to a musical theatre role will suggest a different avenue, and *some* different attributes, from one where a deeper study of performing arts at degree level is wished for.

Opportunities

Early experiences in this sector often occur at school or with youth groups. Many performers find themselves niches of some kind in the vast area *between* those modest but important beginnings, and starring in long runs of famous shows in London and on Broadway. Opportunities may extend from working in a revue, with only three or four colleagues, to having major or minor roles in large-scale productions. There are, of course, several sectors of work in this field that do not require personal performance in public, for example, design, production and lighting, much of which is computerized.

Training

Colleges, conservatoires and universities offering recognized courses provide most of the specialist musicians who make a solid living as performers in the 'classical' arena, but it is possible either to work 'across' the arts after a sharply-focused main training, or to concentrate on one area after a more broadly-based arts degree. First-study musicians contemplating Performing Arts courses should establish the extent of individual tuition in that study. This can be costly to arrange if it is not offered within the course.

Much of the training for stage roles in music/theatre/dance takes place prior to the traditional 18–21 age period and normally attracts a discretionary award. Pursuing such a course independently can be very expensive (fees as well as living costs for up to three years). You should not assume that acceptance by an independent arts training school will necessarily mean a grant from your Local Authority (**see page 5**). You may wish to find the answers to the following questions.

- If the course does not attract a mandatory grant what will be the overall cost? (See above, plus spending money, examination fees etc.)
- If I audition for an award without success, may I re-audition the next year?
- What is the success rate in finding jobs (and of what kind) after the course?
- How 'marketable' is the end-qualification – is it recognized for teaching, for further courses, or training by an employer?

If you are auditioning for grants or jobs for music-theatre and similar stage training with singing, even as a second study, you should take regular lessons in that beforehand, and ensure that any accompaniment (especially if you use a cassette) is well prepared and in a suitable key. It is sometimes helpful if the style of your singing piece contrasts with your dance or theatre extract.

At undergraduate level, De Montfort, Nottingham Trent and Middlesex universities list BA degrees in Performing Arts or similar. Other HE institutions offer combinations including links with Leisure and Tourism studies. (This link will also be found within GNVQs.)

There is an extremely helpful book – *Working in a Performing Company* – sponsored by BP and published by the Royal Opera House. It has a useful loose-leaf format, costs about £12.50 and is available from their Education Department, Covent Garden, London WC2 9DD. There is very full coverage of all aspects of performing (including ballet), production and administration – 40 staff were interviewed.

Conducting

The job

The work involves directing performances of all kinds of music, in various locations, by participants numbering from just a few to many hundreds. The conductor's intention must be to re-create the composer's work faithfully and enthusiastically, to fashion a persuasive as well as stylish performance.

Skills and abilities required

The conductor must understand people and their abilities, to encourage them to give more than they thought possible in the work's realization. It is vital to know a great deal about the construction of works, the human voice and the capabilities of instruments. Orchestral players will ask a number of questions about bowing and phrasing, singers about pronunciation and breathing, all of which need to be answered confidently. This assurance comes only through experience together with detailed knowledge and preparation of the score (and parts). If they are accepting direction in a performance, the participants have a right to expect this preparation – many performers will have been involved in the work more often than the conductor. It is unlikely that a conductor will proceed far without a well-developed artistic sense, a very acute musical ear and good keyboard skills.

If you make headway as a conductor, try to make your concerts as attractive as possible, with soloists, and opportunities for the audience to socialize. Also, when you have something special in a programme, invite former tutors, critics and others whom you wish to impress with your progress and maturing skills. Set about familiarizing yourself with a great deal of music (one famous conductor said to a promising student, 'Come back when you know well 1000 works,') and go to as many rehearsals as you are allowed to attend.

Few conductors are able to spend their whole working life exclusively with professional musicians. Most, therefore, need the advantage of easy adaptation to the expectations of enthusiastic amateur choirs, youth orchestras and semi-professional groups, all of whom need to see the experienced professional conductor change to the encouraging trainer and back in varying degrees. By no means all conductors have this ability.

Many conductors in the entertainment media – usually called **musical directors** (MDs) – need to be able to listen intently through headphones and watch closely through closed-circuit television (CCTV), as some of their performers may not be in the same studio. Opera houses also use the closed-circuit facility.

Opportunities

You have to create opportunities, by persuading people to join you in the expectation of a satisfying and enjoyable set of well-prepared rehearsals and performances. Very little conducting work comes the way of young people still in training, other than that which they organize for themselves. As skills such as baton technique and orchestral score-reading develop, and practical experience is gained, some students may gain access to seminars and more substantial coursework, and the thinking behind particular interpretations. Student performances promoted by the college may flow from this, but you will have to organize most of your conducting yourself. A number of conductors have been distinguished orchestral players at an earlier stage, thus observing many of the finest musical directors at first hand. Some work predominantly in one sector such as ballet, opera, film or TV and stage shows. In the last two of these, considerable skill as an arranger is frequently expected. A number of young conductors come to prominence as prize-winners in competitions, where the rewards are engagements with established choirs, orchestras or opera groups.

Training

Most conservatoires offer conducting courses but, as these vary in duration and the point at which the student may specialize, further enquiries should be made. The National Opera Studio accepts post-diploma répétiteurs from time to time. Although some advice can be given regarding technical matters, the personality of the conductor, and his or her musical integrity, will be of cardinal importance in the leadership of a group of performers. Whatever training is undertaken, openings must be sought, and performances given which may lead to other invitations, such as work with established youth and amateur orchestras, chorus coaching, deputy, and répétiteur positions. Since Britain has few opera houses, conductors with that interest may need to seek part of their training abroad.

Making your way in the pop/rock world

Some general advice for bands and singer/songwriters

Many musicians perform in these and a rich variety of non-classical fields. The following suggestions apply widely.

- Be critical about your band's standards, particularly in your own compositions.
- Establish as strong a local following as possible. To be confident that 40–50 people will regularly support you is important in securing gig bookings. Think about leaflets, posters, T-shirts – they all help in convincing people of your determination.
- If you are sending examples of your work to others, use a recording studio (or create one yourselves) for your demonstration tape/CD.
- Make sure that other aspects of your communication (examples of handbills, brief covering note) are neat and well-presented.
- Limit your submission to three items, with some contrast of style, and mark each clearly on the box and cassette/CD.
- Make contact with local radio stations.
- When you feel that you are working at a high level of competence, try to attract the attention of a particular person in the **Artists and Repertoire** (A and R) department of a recording company. These people are very important in deciding which artists are taken on. A large company may have six or seven members in its A and R team.

Videos are currently very much part of this scene. Many acts are now on computer disks. The Rock School has established a set of graded examinations – see *Appendix 2: Some additional notes* (**page 103**).

Opportunities

Magazines such as *Melody Maker* and *New Musical Express* include advertisements from bands wanting individual players and singers, and vice versa. (Be cautious when replying to advertisements that ask for money to be deposited up front for agency-type services.) Otherwise, it's very much up to you to create the chances to perform, gather regular fans and widen the circuit of venues.

Some performers have found the short courses on recording studios and techniques helpful. Details of a useful book on home recording studios are included in *Decision-making at 18+* (**page 11**).

As work comes in, it brings with it related jobs for **managers**, who look after the business side and deal with companies, **agents**, who try to secure gigs, and **promoters**. The last:

- promote **bands** in a particular venue, take the money, pay the performers and have all the hirer's usual responsibilities
- promote **records,** which is different and is covered on **page 94**.

Your own compositions

Copyright can be a cause of concern. Two major institutions deal with this.

- The Performing Rights Society (PRS), as one of its roles, seeks to gain the proper income for composers when their works are performed on radio stations and in public halls.
- The Mechanical Copyright Protection Society (MCPS) takes on a similar role when compositions are recorded.

They will advise if required. You can take basic simple precautions such as marking manuscripts and cassettes clearly with the symbol © and your name and the date before you send them anywhere. Further proof may be provided by sending yourself a copy of the cassette and/or music – duly marked with copyright details – through the post and *not opening it* when it arrives. This establishes the date of composition.

Jeff Rich, *Status Quo*'s drummer is quoted as saying, after a long and varied career that includes working in special schools, *'Hard work, determination and good luck are important aspects of success in the music business, alongside being versatile and having a broad outlook.'*

Case study: **Matthew**

Matthew, an excellent trumpeter and singer at school (he sang Sarastro in *The Magic Flute)* has a degree in Music from the University of East Anglia. There he played in bands of various styles and eventually 'fell into' one with a fairly 'poppy' style based in London. Two of the members then left – an accepted hazard for small groups in all styles of music performance – leaving him and a colleague to work at writing and performing, sending demo tapes to recording companies and developing contacts. This partner then secured a contract on his own.

By this time well experienced, Matthew replied to an advertisement in *Melody Maker* and spent two successful years as a keyboard player, mainly touring in a support rock band (very nearly securing a substantial employment deal). More recently he has formed a duo with the singer of the original rock band; the bass and drums are computer-programmed. They have secured niches in a number of venues which are not licensed for a normal five-piece group and have also played several times in Portugal and Finland.

The sequence sets out an interesting pathway from traditional music education to a role in the band world, shows the need to remain optimistic through the changes of both fortune and personnel, and the wisdom of seeking more than one source of income. For a band, much of the work will come via a successful manager. For a smaller group, the role of an agent in securing 'gigs' and tours becomes more important.

Composing and Performing, pillars of the National Curriculum in Music for school pupils, live on in the jungle of the commercial band world!

Playing opportunities in the Armed Services

The job

The work involves playing in bands and other musical ensembles based on regiments and Royal Marine establishments while on enlistment. Postings may entail service abroad and on ship. Alongside comprehensive musical training, general education and military subjects will be taught. There are various lengths of compulsory engagement (from 18 this may be as little as three years) and rates of pay.

Skills and abilities required

Skills required at entry differ. For example, the RAF asks for Grade 8, and tends to recruit at 20+ rather than 16. These skills will need to be complemented by soundness of character and a willingness to respond to a certain amount of discipline. More specific qualities are needed for progression to **Bandmaster** training. These will include those required for conducting (**see pages 40–41**), plus knowledge of the capabilities of all instruments, the ability to orchestrate and arrange, and imagination to show off the band in its best light for a variety of occasions and venues, frequently out of doors.

The Royal Marines usually require their musicians to become good at two instruments during training; other services are less insistent. Ability to play in different styles of music is a definite asset for a candidate and the training gives an advantage to the service person. Clearly, the predominant activity is in wind, brass and percussion.

Opportunities and training

There are several attractions for musicians in the Armed Services, apart from loan of instruments, expert tuition and the possibility of foreign travel. Services groups often broadcast, play at major sporting occasions, and divide into smaller groups for important social events. Training is given in band leadership and management, and possibilities exist for promotion. Encouragingly, the proportion of female musicians in the services is rising.

A certain amount of reorganization of Services music training is in hand.

Useful addresses

Further information on entry is available from:

- *The RAF School of Music,* Uxbridge, Middlesex UB10 0R2 (telephone 01895 237144, extension 6286)
- *The Royal Military School of Music,* Kneller Hall, Twickenham, Middlesex TW2 7DU (telephone 0181 898 5533, extension 8638)
- *The Royal Marines School of Music,* HMS *Nelson*, Queen Street, Portsmouth (telephone 01705 722351).

Teaching

Teaching music in the classroom

The job

In nursery, infant and junior classes, music is often taught by the teacher responsible for most areas of the curriculum for that class, sometimes assisted by a music co-ordinator. There may be a visiting specialist. Secondary schools generally have one or more speciality-trained teachers who can take pupils through to the public examinations and into higher education. All teaching in state-maintained schools must comply with pupils' National Curriculum entitlements up to age 14 (Expressive Arts 5–14 in Scotland). Currently the Attainment Targets cover *Performing and composing* and *Listening and appraising*. The job entails planning appropriate activities and organizing resources for these. Pupils' musical development and progress need to be assessed and recorded. Many teachers organize extended curriculum activities such as bands, ensembles and choral groups, and need to liaise with visiting instrumental staff, so that pupils' total music activities have coherence.

Skills and abilities required

A successful teacher will be a good communicator, competent in musical and pedagogic skills. Enthusiasm for and an understanding of young people, their interests and learning development will be essential. An ability to organize schemes of work and visiting staff are just as crucial. Music learning will need to be seen as primarily participative, having many cross-curricular applications. Class teachers in state schools will hold qualifications accepted by the Department for Education and Employment (**see page 13**).

Opportunities

There are opportunities for teachers to be promoted above the basic scale to posts of responsibility; these vary according to the size of school. Some music teachers develop their careers through pastoral posts, co-ordinator roles, or leadership of joint arts teaching teams. Others may become involved in supervisory work at a music centre, take on other responsibilities in the local community or seek a move into the advisor-inspector teams.

Training

See *Decision-making at 18+* (**page 10**), *Postgraduate courses* (**page 20**) and the *Career pathways at 18+* diagram (**page 17**). Successful completion of teacher-training gives **Qualified Teacher Status**. (Independent schools may not require this.) Teachers need to keep their knowledge and skills up to date, via courses and other aspects of professional development.

As more pupils with **special needs** are integrated into mainstream education, all teachers need to have the confidence and understanding to work with and encourage them. Schools should provide in-house training appropriate to the disability. There are always new challenges in this area, for example, there is increasing interest in how pupils with a Specific Learning Difficulty (Dyslexia) tackle laterality and aural concepts – left-right/high-low – and sequencing, which form such a critical part of music-reading, hand placement and the relation of eye, hand and ear. Much research is also being done into how various parts of the brain react to music.

Instrumental teaching in schools

The job

Teachers are engaged either full-time or part-time, on contracts or paid on an hourly basis, and often teach in several schools during a week. This may involve individual and group lessons, and there are sometimes opportunities to direct ensembles, bands and orchestras. Most instrumental teaching arrangements cover orchestral instruments and guitar, some the piano/keyboards and recorder. Steel pans and instruments from other cultures are also often available.

The instrumental teacher may be a member of a team working for the LEA Music Service or similar system but will need to relate closely to the teacher in charge of music in a school. The collaboration of class music staff and instrumental and singing colleagues implies a mutual understanding of the contribution each makes to individual pupils' total music development. (**See also page 46.**)

Skills and abilities required

Instrumental teachers in LEA-maintained schools are expected to hold an appropriate specialist qualification. A high level of competence and ability to demonstrate this are required, together with enthusiasm and the energy to form relationships with a number of pupils, staff and schools. There will be a need to understand both the newer arrangements for funding instrumental tuition in schools, and the inter-relation of this work with the other music curriculum contexts. Preparation of pupils for grade examinations is likely to be required. A knowledge of appropriate materials and repertoire, of how pupils learn, and various teaching strategies is essential.

Opportunities

Opportunities may arise to gain promotion to responsibilities for projects, developments and supervision of instrumental staff in an area of LEA. Independent schools may offer an extensive commitment as part of the main music staff. Teachers may also be involved in group or section coaching on an area basis for holiday or one-day courses.

Training

Most instrumental teachers working in schools will have attended a conservatoire, but a university or college of higher education path is equally possible. Many will seek Qualified Teacher Status by some route and this will give opportunities for teaching practice.

See *Decision-making at 18+: Teaching* (**page 13**) for new developments regarding other entry requirements (including non-music GCSEs), and also *Postgraduate courses* (**page 20**). Well established and supportive specialist associations include, for example, the European String Teachers' Association (ESTA) and LEAs usually provide a variety of in-service training. The Associated Board of the RSM has developed courses assisting professional development. These one-year part-time courses are regionally-based.

As emphasized elsewhere, the teaching profession needs to attract the best musicians!

Private teaching

Private teaching is carried out largely on a self-employed basis.

The job

Many musicians teach individual – or sometimes groups of – pupils, in the teacher's own home, in a studio or (rarely) in the homes of their pupils. Sometimes this teaching is combined, on a part-time basis, with another musical activity, maybe performing, composing or teaching in a school. The job involves giving advice and guidance to the pupils on technical aspects of the instrument or voice, ensuring that the student achieves the necessary skills to develop competence, suggesting the repertoire and giving general encouragement. If the teaching is at home, a pleasant and reasonably spacious environment is important. The teaching normally involves preparation for grade examinations and, possibly, for festivals and competitions, or entry to conservatoires and other higher education.

Skills and abilities required

Most teachers acquire pupils by establishing a reputation, sometimes as a performer. A specialist teaching diploma or qualification is not essential, but most prospective pupils will choose to receive lessons from a teacher with such a qualification. Executant skills to a high standard on the instrument or voice are expected, and teachers should have a sympathetic understanding of their pupils' development in musical studies in order to offer guidance and encouragement.

This support may include organization of master classes or other events where pupils of the same teacher can perform to a friendly audience.

Opportunities

The opportunity to develop this line of work, full- or part-time, depends much on reputation and the teachers' skills in developing pupils' talents over a long period. Some teachers like to combine private teaching with involvement in music centres or schools to achieve variety of venue and to meet with other music colleagues.

Training

Most private teachers will have completed training at a conservatoire or elsewhere in the higher education sector, and some will have established their clientele after completing an external diploma of a conservatoire. Latterly, both the Associated Board of the RSM and Trinity College of Music have developed courses specifically to assist private teachers in enhancing teaching skills.

Many music teachers belong to a long-established professional association – The Incorporated Society of Musicians (ISM) – which publishes a number of pamphlets giving advice, including recommended levels of fees. It organizes conferences and provides a scheme of professional development jointly with Reading University.

Examining and adjudicating

Most young musicians encounter examiners through grade examinations. Some of them may be rather forbidding, but generally they are friendly and concerned that you do your best! Examiners have to be widely experienced, prepared to travel extensively (perhaps abroad for three months at a time) and maintain a consistent standard of marking through a high variation of performance quality across most instruments and voices. Over 150 candidates a week may be heard. Examiners who assess scripts rather than performances also have a heavy load of marking.

Training for examiners has to be an important and ongoing feature, so that marking standards can be consistent, both within the UK and with centres abroad.

An important variation of this type of work, that entails more visiting of schools and colleges, is **external examining** or **moderating**. This can mean casting a practised eye over a sample of candidates' work for GCSE, A/AS level, diploma or degree, to agree gradings or hearing practical tests.

Another related activity involves adjudicating, from modest house competitions in schools, to those of national interest like the BBC *Young Musician of the Year* and international prizes and awards. The three important differences from straightforward examining are:

- the absence of a standardized marking scheme
- the possibility of a panel rather than an individual making the decision
- the judgement being made under the public's scrutiny.

Establishing a clear winner and sometimes rank order is crucial.

Examiners and adjudicators are drawn from experienced musicians in all branches of the profession.

Combining teaching and performing

The cross-fertilization available through this combination can be of great benefit to pupils, who feel a direct contact with the professional music world through their teacher, but it needs to be very carefully and sensitively organized. It is to be hoped that all who teach will seek some training in the art.

Potentially the plan can work as well for those young professionals anxious to make their way in the freelance world, taking part-time work in schools and music centres, as for well-known players and singers teaching in colleges, universities and conservatoires. The essentially rigorous nature of school and college timings (not least regarding pupils' own timetables) and availability of accommodation, are the factors which can limit flexibility.

Post-18 students are more able to cope with an occasional two- or three-week gap in tutoring than are young instrumentalists in school. It is not surprising that Heads of Music find it difficult to deal with frequent changes of visiting-days, and it may be even more frustrating when the performer is offered a long-awaited series of engagements.

This is a real dilemma – whether to take a substantial teaching post or to leave yourself free to accept the majority of professional engagements which are offered. The emphasis can be changed, with some degree of luck, on an annual basis, but it is important for all concerned to realize that sensible professional concert-planning means that the single rehearsal-and-concert engagement is becoming rarer and the requirement is more likely to be for some days.

Given infinite flexibility this combination of activity will work admirably. Other compromises which can be fulfilling include the following.

- The high-level 'semi-professional' involvement of school teaching staff in local performances where the timings of performances and rehearsals are convenient. Proximity to large urban areas can give opportunities for work of a high standard. Stage shows will produce more income, but can be accumulatively tiring!
- The 'residency', largely founded by universities taking on ensembles in the 1960s. This allows the group time to rehearse and prepare for its own professional performances, and requires teaching commitment in return.
- Seeking as much professional performance as possible but honouring a small amount of teaching e.g. in a LEA music centre or conservatoire Saturday Junior Exhibitioner arrangements.

Composing

Composing

The job

It is seldom realized quite how widely composition skills are required in the community in general. Obvious examples range from the professional composer of operas, symphonies and concert works of all kinds, to the professional composer of pop and rock music, or the one who works continuously in the areas of commercials and library music. Then again, the so-called 'amateur' composer, e.g. a school teacher or even someone in a full-time job completely separate from the musical world, may have to write a carol for the local church, a piece for the local brass band, a school musical, songs for their own pop group or jazz ensemble, or incidental music for a play production. The use of music by the consumer, i.e. the community, is vast, and this fact is relatively unappreciated, though it should be added that the opportunities for full-time employment purely as a composer are limited.

Skills and abilities required

Composing takes commitment and self-discipline (e.g. the ability to concentrate for long periods of time on compositional work), including the enthusiasm to accomplish routine checks to ensure immaculate presentation of material. It also demands reliability (the ability to produce the work on time – in legible musical handwriting – and accuracy!) and versatility: the composer must be able to tackle totally different disciplines (theatre, symphonic music, music for education, music for TV video and film, etc.) and disparate musical styles. A 'good ear' is essential. Composers need to be able to get on with people, at the same time being able to cut themselves off from distraction when necessary, but they must be sympathetic to the needs of performers and able to communicate directly with those who are using their music. The ability to adjust between bouts of frequent travel and prolonged periods at home, probably mostly spent in one room working at the compositions, and resilience – coming back kicking after disappointments – are important. Performing (preferably pianistic) and conducting ability are helpful.

Opportunities

To some extent, this is covered above, i.e. use in the community often derives from composers being in positions where their compositional skills can be drawn upon. Opportunities are to some extent also created in the commercial as well as in the 'art' areas, by self-promotion, i.e. sending cassettes, CDs, scores or disks, according to how best any interested parties can evaluate your work. If you are sending only an aural example, it is best also to have a hard copy to hand for reference. In the concert field there exist many organizations devoted to promoting the young composer, e.g. the Society for Promotion of New Music (SPNM).

The British Music Information Centre is a useful source of advice, and the composers' organizations – the Association of Professional Composers (APC), the Composers' Guild of Great Britain – can also advise. The APC in particular, though an organization of purely professional composers, covers the entire spectrum of compositional skills, so can advise about more potential 'markets'. The *British Music Yearbook* is an invaluable source of information and addresses.

Training

There will always be some composers who succeed without moving through traditional routes – those who are lucky enough to find a niche in commercial music may be examples. However, the majority will want to explore the following familiar types of course.

The four Royal Schools of Music, the Birmingham Conservatoire, the Welsh College of Music and Drama (Cardiff) and, in London, Trinity College, the London College of Music and Guildhall School of Music and Drama all offer composition courses – application for a copy of the prospectus should produce the relevant information, but further detailed information can always be requested. Similarly, the prospectuses of university music departments should be studied – some have achieved eminence in the field of composition studies, though sometimes this has concentrated on one area (e.g. concert music) rather than being more general.

The relationship between colleges and universities must also be borne in mind – the regime of one might not be suited to some cases, but better suited to others. Colleges of further/higher education also, in some instances, offer distinguished composition courses, though here the special emphasis (derived from the former status of many of them as teacher training colleges) may again offer a slightly different approach.

In investigating such courses, several points should be considered. First, in so far as it is possible to tell, the particular student's own special interests may suit one kind of curriculum better than another. Second, the extent to which composition studies permeate the college rather than being shunted off into a corner must, if possible, be discovered: a glance at the list of teachers might help to determine the way the institution approaches this. Third, there should be opportunities for student composers to have their works performed, just as there should be opportunities for performers to take part in such performances and in 20th-century music in general. In terms of exposure to public concert-giving, it is obvious that those establishments in the big cities have immediate advantages, but it must be carefully considered whether a more rural or less metropolitan setting does not offer other compensations for particular kinds of composition study.

If you are a young composer still at school your teacher may seek access to expert coaching internally; this should be found at – or through – a local music centre. From time to time the Regional Arts Boards may have a Composer in Residence scheme available in your area. Although this is unlikely to provide regular lessons over a long period, any such opportunity should be taken.

John McCabe, composer, pianist (and former Director of London College of Music)

Useful addresses

- *The Society for the Promotion of New Music* (SPNM), Francis House, Francis Street, London SW1 1DE (telephone 0171 828 9696).
- *Sonic Arts Network,* at the same address as SPNM, is an association of composers, performers and teachers developing the creative uses of technology in composing and performing, and integrating this with classroom resources. Its main telephone number is 0171 828 9796 (Education Director 01438 359344).

Arranging

Nearly every musician makes arrangements. This is what is happening when a primary school youngster plays a familiar tune on a xylophone and – more clearly the case – when a music teacher works out a version of a folk-song for the particular group in hand or a candidate makes one in the composition sector of the GCSE examination.

Professional arrangers are a rare breed. There is a very special skill in working confidently across various styles, with one eye on the original composition (not all scores for music-theatre are fully laid out by the composer), another on the requirements of the commission, and yet a third on providing a stylish, performable and memorable outcome!

Considerable experience as an orchestrator or choral arranger, music director (and probably composer) is required. The copyright laws need close attention in this area of work and most professional arrangements are harnessed via publishers, broadcasting and recording companies.

Music technology and composing

Recent developments of hardware and software have put technology even more firmly at the service of composers, from the youngster in primary school to the established professional. All can avoid the important but boring aspect of preparing the performers' materials; they can exchange paper and pencil for screen and interface, so that note information can be converted into easily-printed scores and parts.

Alongside this, advances in recording, storing and replaying musical material have created the situation where both **recording studio engineer** and **composer** can work with the same equipment, although for different musical ends. Composers can change the material in a variety of ways before replaying. The more radical transformations of material have created entirely new sound worlds and musical languages, ranging from more traditional modes through rock and jazz to leading-edge street-cultures such as **hip hop**, **ambient**, **jungle** and **trance**.

Many students leaving school will have experience in using score-writing facilities, in packages which also enable **orchestration with MIDI**. In this system, performance material from electronically-generated sounds and samples imitating acoustic instruments can be edited and replayed or saved to digital media. Latterly, a few may also have been able to combine MIDI recordings with 'hard disk' recording. This allows real sounds to be changed into digital format, stored, edited and replayed from a computer's hard disk, and promises to offer the most comprehensive tools for transforming or **sculpting sound**. The combination of advanced editing facilities and 'live' processing features offers composers an almost unlimited palette of sounds, undreamt of possibilities for structuring compositions, and combinations of acoustic elements, live-processed and pre-crafted material.

This progress means that a student moving to a music degree course should expect to find access not only to high quality **recording** facilities, but also to digital **composing** support which allows advanced manipulation of sound sources.

Fortunately, as these advances are made, sophisticated equipment tends to become more affordable. Clearly, if you are investing in it because it will help your musical career, thorough investigation is crucial. Take plenty of advice in order to assemble what is right for you.

Remember that the technology can work wonders and respond to your imagination but it's the quality of your musical thought that will be the crucial factor.

Preparing music for the screen

Advances in music technology have naturally had their effect on music for the screen, where a number of considerations (including budget) will determine whether the music is made directly via one or two keyboard/synthesizers or a large orchestra.

The composer needs special skills – whether or not the music will be performed by a group of musicians in the studio – of crafting the music to a meticulously-timed series of short paragraphs. It may be that the music has to make its mark in a very short time, for example for an advertisement or brief video. A full-length film will make different demands.

If the music track is laid by players and/or singers in the studio, there needs to be a conductor or leader (maybe the composer) scrupulous about the speed of these episodes, to synchronize the track with the visual action. The music cue sheet will have the film's footage listed and timed – down to small parts of a second – against the action, and the conductor's score will also have some of these indicated. In order to achieve synchronization, all performers will have access via headsets to a 'click-track' (in effect an electronic metronome) but will also be able to hear each other.

However the music is created, the composer will have been in discussion early in the project about where the music must make its greatest impact. However, only at the dubbing and mixing stage will it be finally clear at what points the music is dominant and where it partly gives way to the other aural tracks such as dialogue and sound effects (often referred to as FX).

Training

For those seeking specific training, there is a postgraduate diploma in Music for Film and TV at London College of Music at Thames Valley University. There is similar postgraduate provision at Bournemouth University, and as part of the University of Westminster degree in Commercial Music.

Education work for professional groups and animateurs

The jobs and skills required

Although they have different starting points, both these areas involve the encouragement of young people's creative abilities through contact with professional artists.

Many professional groups, including opera houses, now pursue a strong education or 'outreach' policy, with a designated officer. This work is interpreted widely, and can involve workshops in prisons as well as schools, hospices and hospitals, with some remarkable and moving results. In the school context, it may mean supervising composing projects. This can be productive both in the school and through links with a work the group is soon to perform locally. Now that these schemes have established themselves, they are also driven by players' and singers' wishes for closer communication in the encouragement of the next century's audiences. The life of the community and the school is enriched by these professional visits, especially if they can be extended to a 'residency' and an exciting final 'performance'.

Audition panels are now very keen to know whether the applicants for playing and singing positions have some experience or interest in this work. There are examples of posts in the list of jobs in music advertised (see *Appendix 1: Jobs in music advertised 1996,* **page 100**).

The role of the **animateur** has emerged recently, combining skills of performer, teacher and organizer in response to local need and support. It is an interactive task, releasing talent and creativity in the community, whether it is enriched by many music traditions or not. A post might involve:

- leading an area project on choral work
- encouraging a greater understanding of, for example, Asian dance
- harnessing professional actors and musicians in workshops and preparation for community music-theatre.

For work of this type, commitment to various styles and music is vital, alongside well-developed communication skills and an understanding of how people can be encouraged to participate in unfamiliar territory, explore other traditions and find commonalities. That unfamiliarity may as easily be of venue – a local prison, hospital or special school – as of style.

As there is frequently a strong community identity, animateur posts are often funded by the local council, possibly in alliance with an appropriate national association.

Opportunities and training

These posts allow positive interaction between professionals and young people. The animateur arrangements will probably be of longer duration (perhaps one year) while an orchestra or opera house outreach programme might have a more intensive effect covering various single visits or short residency over a term.

Several attempts are now being made in higher education to break down unnecessary barriers between performer and audience. The Music Performance and Communication Skills course at the Guildhall School of Music and Drama has led the way in providing training and development for musicians to be responsive to changing social and musical – as well as educational – needs within the community. Some animateurs will have taken Combined or Performing Arts training.

Sometimes, our own methods of music learning have been too narrowly based. A young pianist was not pleased to have this criticism on New Year's Eve: 'How is it that you've had music training for three years but you can't play "Auld Lang Syne"?'

Case study: **Richard McNichol**

This case study is included as one example of a well-established professional musician whose career has changed course but who remained dedicated to music education.

I started my professional life as a school teacher. I had taken a degree in Music and had stayed at university as a research graduate. Quite suddenly my grant ran out. This was totally unexpected and I did not know which way to turn. In those days, you were a qualified teacher by virtue of having a degree and I returned to my home town, Nottingham, and started teaching the following week in a boys' comprehensive school.

Whilst at university I had played the flute in the university orchestra and had visited London every month or so to take flute lessons with a principal player in one of the London orchestras. I continued to visit London from Nottingham for very occasional lessons, and on one of these occasions my teacher asked me if I would like to become a professional player. His offer was that if I were prepared to move to London, he would give me one concert in the flute section of the BBC Symphony Orchestra and I could see how life progressed from there. My wife and I were prepared to take the risk and we moved to London.

To earn a living whilst not playing the flute (which was most of the time) I struck a deal with Haringey Local Authority. I agreed to teach on a supply basis in any school, any subject, provided that in return the Authority would release me at no notice to accept any engagement playing the flute that I might get. This arrangement worked extremely amicably for a year, most of which I spent teaching. At the end of the year, I was offered the job of playing the flute in a West End musical, and on the strength of this I ended my arrangement with Haringey.

The initial engagement with the BBC Symphony Orchestra had led to spasmodic and widely-spaced engagements with the other London orchestras. If somebody fell ill at short notice, or if the orchestra needed a larger number of flutes than its normal complement I, amongst others, was invited to work with them. The rest of my early playing career consisted of a motley selection of Parks' dates (sight-read bandstand concerts of extraordinarily indifferent standard), engagements with ad hoc orchestras for everything from a symphonic repertoire to accompanying local amateur opera groups, extremely occasional pop sessions, private teaching and any form of playing that came my way. In the early years I literally turned nothing away, and the experience gained from this constant change of environment proved invaluable throughout my later playing career.

I gradually found myself in the fortunate position of having first refusal on the extra work of three of the London orchestras. At a time of relatively ample funding, this proved an extremely full-time job. It took me around the world on orchestral tours whilst giving me the freedom, should I wish to do something else, to say no to the orchestra that offered me the engagement. I found this a highly satisfactory way of life and had little intention of ever becoming a permanent member of any orchestra. However, the London Philharmonic Orchestra invited me to join them as second flute, and as the first flute and the piccolo player had been close friends throughout my playing career, the offer was too attractive to refuse.

These were halcyon years for being in the London Philharmonic Orchestra. The conducting line-up was dazzling – Barenboim, Haitink, Solti, Boult, Pritchard, Giulini ...

As a freelance player, I had always been heavily involved in chamber orchestras and chamber music. I played in a wind quintet called the *Athena Ensemble* and a mixed quartet call the *Apollo Ensemble*. Whenever these groups undertook music club engagements, we offered to do a school concert at the same time. I always enjoyed these tremendously – often more than the evening concerts. I found it easy to communicate with children, I enjoyed their sense of humour, their freshness and their enthusiasm. We did children's concerts with the big orchestras too. In general, however, these were abysmally presented, often containing totally unsuitable music, and usually promoted to gratify the ambition of the conductor or would-be conductor involved. Professional players detested these engagements – the most common statement made by the professional player being that 'this should put another audience off for life'.

By 1977 I felt strongly enough about this state of affairs to decide to organize some children's concerts of my own that were truly educationally based. I approached Marks & Spencer and asked for a sum of money to mount a pilot scheme of workshops for children, to be given with 12-string players. My plan was to involve the children in playing with the little orchestra, in creating their own music, in exploring various aspects of music, and generally being as actively involved in the process as possible. It also seemed important to me that these workshops provided a stimulus and material for the teacher to continue the work in the classroom. Marks & Spencer gave me the money on condition that I founded a charitable trust, and the *Apollo Trust* was born. I approached the ILEA who agreed to circulate their schools to raise audiences for the projected series. The response from the ILEA junior schools was excellent and the project went from strength to strength over the course of four years. It was a modest project, consisting only of four workshops spaced at monthly intervals over the autumn and spring terms. As a result of interest created by this series, I was approached by the English Sinfonia to devise an extended educational project which would be funded by the Arts Council of Great Britain. By the time this project had run for a year, I was faced with the choice of either taking six months' leave from the LPO to complete the educational concerts I was now being offered, or to tender my resignation. I gave six months' notice and left at the end of Glyndebourne in the Summer of 1982.

Educational projects and concerts now occupy my entire life and I enjoy working across the whole field, from classroom (including of course SEN schools) to the concert hall. After leaving the LPO I was invited to initiate orchestral education work with most of the British orchestras and in 1992 became Music Animateur with the London Symphony Orchestra, an orchestra with such commitment to the ideal of orchestras as an educational resource that we have recently made *Music Explorer*, a 90-minute video conducted by Sir Colin Davis to help teachers to teach classroom music throughout Britain and the world.

British music education is widely regarded as the finest in the world. I have worked with teachers and their pupils in Germany, Austria, Spain, France, Norway, Sweden, Finland, Iceland, Jordan, the USA and Canada, all eager to adopt the British model.

World musics

The jobs

Full-time jobs in less well-known musical traditions are not easy to iden-tify, except for those as leaders of specialist organizations and recording companies with this emphasis, and the relatively few established ensem-bles. Musicians following the more familiar career paths must be more than just aware of other cultures and the enrichment that they bring. Study of these is now more frequently required for public examinations, bringing greater awareness of the commonalities as well as distinctive aspects. Most of us are still on a steep learning curve and 'playing and listening is better than just reading about'.

World musics start close at hand, for example musicians involved in Irish and Welsh traditional material are just as much part of it as their colleagues in Turkey, China and Japan.

Everyone who has any kind of teaching position plays an important role in promoting wider understanding of these cultures, as there are so many different approaches to the Arts. Some traditions wish to see instruments taught in the temple rather than school or music centre. Others do not favour full involvement in certain kinds of music, and a concert hall or theatre is not always an appropriate place for the per-formance.

It is critical to seek authentic performances and recordings, and to be wary of imitations and parodies that often occur in the media.

Opportunities

In the UK, there are relatively few established professional ensembles in this field. They can sometimes secure a series of performances, possibly supported by bodies such as the National Arts Councils. For most others, unless accepted as a practitioner into one of these ensembles (rare), first contact with the less familiar traditions and timbres is often likely to be through hands-on access to ethnic instruments. You might wish to assemble and demonstrate a collection yourself. Although you are unlikely to achieve personal ownership of a Javanese *gamelan*, gather-ing enough examples to illustrate African drumming, or to know your *shofar* from your *shakuhachi* might be feasible. You might become good at arranging and directing music for steel pans. Above all, involve expert practitioners wherever you can.

In a different sphere, clearer insights have recently been shown into Bhangra music, which owes much to the Sikh traditions of north-west India and has a strong following amongst some groups of young people. There are many bands, and musicians also often play for weddings – the bridegroom chooses the music – and occasionally even for Muslim and Hindu ceremonies.

Training

Some ethnic communities are developing centres for instruction, where teachers or gurus offer advice and guidance. The Bhavan Centre in West London is an example. Interestingly, 15 per cent of its students are not Asian. Specialist organizations include World of Music and Dance – WOMAD – (materials and specialist recordings) and Aklowa (African drumming). Details of these are in *Appendix 3: Useful addresses* (**page 104**). There is an important audio-visual archive in the School of Oriental and African Studies (SOAS) in the University of London, and a large collection of African and Asian instruments at the Royal College of Music.

Other training includes courses combining academic and practical work in this field. King Alfred's College, Winchester has a modular BA in World Musics, and at Dartington College, Devon, these studies form an important part of the degree. Both have *gamelan*, as do York University, the Bate Collection in Oxford and the South Bank Centre, London. Several other higher education institutions, including SOAS, list ethnomusicology (the study of music of different cultures) as course components.

Music therapy

The job

Choosing a career as a music therapist is one option that is available to musicians seeking work in the community. Music as therapy is now establishing itself as a discipline in its own right with a wide range of clinical applications. This is not a career to be chosen lightly, as it demands a high degree of both musicianship and motivation. A mature approach is needed to work with people of all ages with any difficultie and problems, particularly in the area of communication. Music thera pists also often work in multi-disciplinary teams, in hospital settings schools and community based-centres and units.

Skills and abilities required

A music therapist needs an enthusiastic interest in music-making at al levels and in many styles. Versatility is also important, since the musi therapist is called upon to adapt to the needs of the individual, whethe this is working one-to-one or in a group. A keen compositional intelli gence is challenged by working with the raw elements of sound and music, e.g. working with single sounds when supporting the music of a person with profound disabilities. Therapists need not be first-stud pianists, though keyboard skills are necessary for the work. String and woodwind players find the use of sustained melody to be very effective

A music therapist must be able to share their music, to want to commu nicate and be willing often to work with very limited responses. Thi means that patience, tolerance, empathy and warmth are needed in plentiful supply. Physical, intellectual and emotional stamina are calle for. Because of this blend of personal and musical qualities, it is often the case that potential therapists enter the field after an early career as, fo example, a performer or teacher.

Opportunities

The career and grading structure within the National Health Servic means that music therapists are paid on a level with other para-medica professions. At present, to work full-time in special schools a musicia normally needs a teacher's certificate. Therapists also work in:

- hospitals for adults with learning difficulties, mental health problems and physical disabilities
- pre-school assessment centres
- units for the elderly
- day nurseries
- the probation service
- centres for the deaf and blind.

Some therapists are contracted for full- or part-time work; some are freelance, offering sessional work, and some combine different jobs, e.g research, teaching, performing with therapy. There is a growing development in research and in working with more community-based groups and charities. There are many opportunities that present themselves to the creative and determined therapist. A lot of the work may need to be set up by the individual therapist who, very often, will be expected to work single-handed.

Training

At present there are four full-time and one part-time postgraduate training courses. For further information and course details write to: The Administrator, British Society for Music Therapy (**address on page 104**). Any musician interested in pursuing the career of a music therapist is advised to join this Society. Further information can also be obtained from The Secretary, Association of Professional Music Therapists in Great Britain (**address on page 104**).

Dr Leslie Bunt, Director of the Music Space Trust, and Music Therapy Training at the University of Bristol, Southville Centre, Beauley Road, Bristol BS3 1QG (telephone 0117 963 8000).

Working with the disabled

The job

In addition to music therapy (**see page 62**), there are several other approaches to working in music with disabled people, some of which have their own relevant training courses. Options include:

- music teaching (instrumental, pre-school, primary/secondary, further education, higher education)
- as a community musician (freelance, or employed by an organization)
- as a performer (live performances in schools, hospitals, day centres)
- within other therapies (speech, therapy, physiotherapy).

In addition, other occupations offer opportunities to specialize in the musical needs of disabled people e.g. audio-visual librarians, arts administration, music publishing, musical instrument repair. These have their own relevant training courses, although disability awareness may not be covered adequately on the courses and so may need to be researched from other sources.

While employment as a music therapist is open only to people having a Diploma of Music Therapy from an approved training course, there are still many musicians working with disabled people in the community who haven't followed an established training route. Consequently, people are often interested in knowing about short courses or workshops which offer ideas and skill-sharing to people interested in – or already working in – the field. In recognizing the growing amount of music opportunities offered to disabled people, an increasing number of music colleges and universities are adding option courses in *Music and disabled people* (see *Training* on **pages 65–6**).

Opportunities

Music education

This can be as an instrumental teacher, or as a music teacher providing a music curriculum within nursery or pre-schools, schools, further education, higher education, conservatoire or in a hospital school. An increasing number of children with disabilities are being integrated into mainstream schools. Therefore, as an alternative to specializing in teaching in special schools, teachers may find themselves teaching music to children with disabilities in ordinary classrooms. Often music and the creative arts are used as a focal point for collaborative work.

The types of disability a student may have are varied – visual, hearing, physical, learning, social/psychological or a hidden disability such as dyslexia or epilepsy. The disability itself may affect the way music is presented or taught, or it can mean consideration of instruments (adaptation or choice of instrument).

Music in the Community

Musicians working in this field may be employed:

- by a community music organization such as Community Music Wales or The Firebird Trust
- by a Local Council as a musician-in-residence
- as a member of a major orchestra or opera company (most now undertake Education/Outreach projects)

or work freelance setting up their own workshops. Over recent years there have been major developments in the community music field, especially in the rise of training courses for musicians wanting to improve skills in this area (see *Training*, below). The work can be in schools, prisons, play groups, residential or day centres, hospitals, public projects, community projects and festivals.

Music performance

People who cannot attend public performances because of severe illness or disability can still enjoy recitals given by visiting performers. Two organizations who audition and engage talented and professional musicians for this work are *Live Music Now!* and the *Council for Music in Hospitals.* This work is usually occasional and part-time. Musicians have to be skilled in presenting well-chosen music in ways that suit their audience – whether they are very ill, have unusual behaviour, are depressed, or unable to communicate through speech.

Music with other therapies

Therapists working in many different disciplines find music of great value. For example:

- physiotherapists may use action songs to encourage body awareness and movement of limbs
- speech therapists use rhythm and melodic line to help the flow of speech and songs to help articulation
- occupational therapists encourage group music activities or use music as an integral part of a reminiscence programme.

Many students who were training to work in these and other professions (including student nurses) and who are interested in music have chosen projects during their training on the use of music in their work. They have then made use of their skills when qualified.

Training

Different courses or training routes relate to different careers or approaches. Details about courses (those leading to qualifications and short courses) are included in the publication *Working in music with disabled people and training available*, from Sound Sense (see address below) as are the following useful publications:

- *Sources of grants and funding*
- *Music and Disability Directory*

Sound Sense now has much of the valuable library and information resource originally assembled by the National Music and Disability Information Service (see also the *Music Education Yearbook*).

Useful addresses

Extensive lists can be found in the above books.

- *Council for Music in Hospitals,* 74 Queens Road, Hersham, Surrey KT12 5LW (telephone 01932 252809/252811)
- *Live Music Now!,* 4 Lower Belgrave Street, London SW1 0LJ (telephone 0171 730 2205)
- *Music and the Deaf,* Brian Jackson Centre, New North Parade, Huddersfield, W Yorkshire (telephone 01484 425551)
- *Royal National Institute for the Blind,* Education Officer, Garrow House, 190 Kensal Road, London W10 5BT (telephone 0181 968 8600)
- *Sound Sense,* the National Community Music Association, Riverside House, Rattlesden, Bury St Edmunds, Suffolk IP30 0SF (telephone 01449 736287)
- *Diploma in Music Teaching in Private Practice,* University of Reading, Dept of Arts & Humanities in Music Education, Bulmershe Court, Earley, Reading, Berkshire RG6 1HY

Laura Crichton, formerly Director, National Music & Disability Information Service (NMDIS)

Case study: **Emma: Community music**

I followed a familiar path at school, doing English, Music and Economics at A level, and played percussion in the County Youth Orchestra.

Since school age, I have maintained a belief that music has the power to create a situation where healthy group interaction and positive individual development can occur.

Whilst I was at Birmingham Conservatoire, where I continued playing percussion, it was clear that there were vast opportunities for student musicians to practise community music, and I became student co-ordinator for the conservatoire's Community Music Scheme. We provided student performers for various establishments, including schools, a day centre for homeless people and residential homes, to give formal and informal concerts. Those students facilitating workshops went to Birmingham Children's Hospital, youth clubs and a day centre for people with learning disabilities.

The students had good performance practice and could develop relevant communication skills, whilst the community groups had live performances and an opportunity to create music themselves.

My 'finals' involved producing a thesis on the differences between community music and music therapy; the discussion lives on within these two disciplines. Community arts practice is often referred to as inclusive or participatory. My own view is that community music looks towards maximizing opportunities for creativity to occur and focuses on sharing and making music (therefore creating the situation about the power of music referred to above). Music therapy arguably looks further and might concentrate on the *effects* of music involvement.

After graduating with a BA Music degree, I worked for Social Services developing a programme of arts activities involving people with learning disabilities. Many sessions took place at the day centre but we had access to premises with the opportunity to use community resources, integrate with a wider society and become fully involved with a participatory arts programme. I applied for education posts with professional orchestras, but am now happily appointed to the new post of Youth and Community Arts Development Officer for a district council.

I have become a committee member of Sound Sense, the National Community Music Association, which has over 200 artists, administrators and others involved in this particularly interesting field of music practice.

Music journalism

The job

Music journalism involves writing, and possibly broadcasting about musical works, their performances and recordings. These reviews and essays could include judgements about composers and performers in all music styles and may appear in newspapers, magazines and books. The hours are often unsociable and extensive travel may be involved, to cover festivals and tours.

The job may involve working for a trade paper, extracting useful information from press releases, and may involve interviews with famous artists. You may have to be persistent in sending examples of your work to papers, journals and magazines. Try to catch – and do a piece on – news directly it breaks.

Skills and abilities required

The main requirement is to be able to write lucidly and evocatively about all kinds of music. This presumes a catholic taste, together with the experience which both assists recognition of an impressive new work through the haze of an unsatisfactory performance (and vice versa) and allows finer distinctions to be drawn between many interpretations, all of which are of a very high order. Requirements of writing style differ; you would not write in the same mode for *Melody Maker* as you would for the *Observer*.

Journalists who cover concert and opera performances have to produce their pieces to a deadline, and for the daily papers this can be a severe one. All writers have to stand by their convictions, and they may have to respond to published disagreements with their views. Aesthetic responses are partly subjective, but have to be credible and constructive when conveyed to others – the success or failure of shows and groups, as well as individuals, can be affected by critics' reviews. There is a knack in writing about music as an art form; it can be different from writing about concerts. All the literary skill in the world is no advantage if the words do not draw the reader towards the music.

Opportunities

Considerable initiative is required for a successful entry into this profession. Full-time posts in journalism are few and exist mainly in the daily and Sunday press, or as editorships of specialist magazines. Much freelance work is done for publications such as *BBC Music* and *Classic FM* magazines, as well as those that review recordings, audio equipment and music technology. Most general magazines have a music 'specialist'. Work may range from previewing or reviewing musical events for a local paper to a scholarly piece about anyone from King David to David Bowie. Syndicated articles, a major assessment of the European jazz scene, work for *Select* or *Q,* or programme notes can all be part of the wide spectrum of music journalism. All writing is subject to editorial abbreviation and availability of space.

Established music journalists receive complimentary tickets for a wide range of events, and reviewers may be able to keep the records and books on which they comment.

Training

Music journalists make their way through widely differing routes although many will have a background of student newspaper or magazine work. Others may have made their mark through the local press. (This will have involved many non-musical assignments.) Some will have started off writing their own fanzines. It may be possible to develop a particular expertise, for example in African music or music technology in education. Some pop journalists also play in bands or act as DJs in clubs – clearly there is an advantage in practising in some way what you are writing about. Whatever you write about needs to be well researched and clearly presented in typescript. You must become familiar with word-processing techniques, and it helps to have access to a fax machine.

A full training programme is available for entrants to newspaper journalism. Good A-level grades are required for both direct entry from school at basic level, and for most higher education courses. The majority of entrants are now graduates. Over 20 colleges around the country offer a variety of courses, including four with journalism itself at first degree level. Postgraduate courses are also available.

Useful address

Further information, including videos, is available from the National Council for the Training of Journalists (NCTJ), Latton Bush Centre, Southern Way, Harlow, Essex CM18 7BL (telephone 01729 430009).

Music librarianship

The job

A music librarian develops and maintains collections of books and printed music, and/or recordings. Users need easy access both to the above and to information surrounding them. The job may also entail facilitating inter-library loans, where one library borrows material, for example a set of *Messiah* chorus parts, from another to satisfy a local request.

Skills and abilities required

The range of technical and managerial skills required includes managing stock, supervising personnel, cataloguing, and data banks. Competition for posts remains keen and successful librarians tend to be well and broadly qualified. They need both core and 'out of the way' knowledge, together with a policy for dealing with someone who brings back an orchestral set with the horn and timpani parts missing.

Opportunities

Public libraries

The majority of professional music librarians work in public libraries. They deal with the widest possible range of users and needs, and often share with record shop assistants the ability to know what 'the music on TV which goes de-da-de, diddi da dum – you know' is! Responsibility for drama collections and audio-visual materials may be theirs. They liaise with schools and youth music groups as well as adult amateur choirs and orchestras, and may need to be alert to other local music collections. A number of Library and Information Assistant posts are available to non-graduates. Progression can be made to higher responsibility via vocational qualifications. Extended opening hours allow part-time work and flexible shifts.

Other specialist libraries

The leading music librarians in national, university and other academic libraries will be able to retain more specialism. They will probably have a music degree, but with a librarianship postgraduate qualification. The position of main qualifications is less clear for those working in colleges and conservatoires but any staff in these five categories may find themselves supervising very important donated collections as well as day-to-day requests. There may be the occasional visit to the auction house.

In broadcasting, orchestral and special music libraries, much will depend on the bias of the post. Orchestral librarians will need to ensure correct bowings and phrasings in the parts, have contact with orchestra members and probably also conductors and soloists. They may contribute to budgeting. Both for this and for a publishing house hire-library (see *Music publishing: Hire librarian*, **page** 75) a music qualification may be important.

In all library posts, there will be contact with publishers and associations involved in copyright. In the last few years, the advances in technology have brought great opportunities to the service regarding information retrieval.

Training and qualifications

Professional librarianship is a graduate profession. The two routes are

- a degree in any subject followed by a postgraduate librarianship diploma or master's degree, or
- a degree in Library and Information Management.

The postgraduate courses usually require up to one year's work experience after degree.

Competition for bursaries for the postgraduate diploma is keen; acceptance for a master's degree may bring a studentship with it.

Useful address

The Library Association is the chartered professional body, accredits degree and postgraduate courses and holds a Graduate Training Opportunities list. It publishes very helpful brochures. The address is:

- The Library Association, 7 Ridgmount Street, London WC1E 7AE (telephone 0171 636 7543).

Music publishing

Music publishing involves much more than the printing and distribution of music or books on the subject. Composers' and authors' interests need protection (copyright has recently been extended from 50 to 70 years in the European Union) and this becomes difficult in these days of easy access to information and the growing use of music in advertisements, cable and satellite television. On-line availability will bring further developments. Commercial risks need to be taken in the printing of and publicity for little-known composers. However, this aspect of the music industry retains a very high and successful profile in this country.

Not all the areas discussed in this Publishing section feature in all publishers, as size of operation and catalogue will dictate what is required. Occupation of one position is not necessarily a stepping-stone to another in the same company, but might well be to a post outside music publishing where similar expertise is sought.

Editor

The job

The role of the editor in music publishing is to ensure that the company acquires the right type of music and music books suitable to its marketing and publishing policy i.e. whether the publisher specializes in pop, classical, middle of the road, educational, vocal, orchestral etc. The editor will examine submitted manuscripts (which are often unsolicited), assess their suitability and, when they *are* accepted, liaise with the production controller in order to proceed to print. The editor will supervise and influence style and layout of the music, commission cover designs, ensure copyright clearances and registrations are progressed, proofread and correct where appropriate and finally ensure that the new music is delivered on time. The editor also provides a liaison between the composer or author and specialist consultants where employed.

NEEDS A

CHIEF SUB EDITOR

The world's best music monthly needs someone to edit, proof-read, caption, headline and assist generally in 'seeing the magazine through' to its heady conclusion each month, working closely with the Production Editor. The ideal candidate will be Quark-savvy, experienced in popular magazines, full of ideas, quick with a quip, mad about music and its attendant cultures, a good team player, self-motivated and an intimate pal of the English language. Knowledge of/familiarity with the music business would be an advantage, but not essential. Writing flair and understanding of what makes Q tick are, however, a prerequisite.

Applications should be sent immediately to **ANDREW COLLINS**, Editor, Q Magazine, EMAP METRO (N), Mappin House, 4 Winsley Street WIN 7AR.

In classical music, the job does not only involve preparing printed books of sheet music for sale; there is also the preparation of performance materials which are hired by orchestras, opera companies, choirs, etc. This kind of work involves highly-skilled processes such as making a piano reduction of the orchestral parts of an opera or choral work for a vocal score.

Skills and abilities required

A musical qualification is usually required (preferably not highly specialized in one area) gained from one of the conservatoires or a university. A catholic taste in music would be an advantage. An ability to work accurately and quickly under pressure against deadlines and an eye for detail are necessary. Diplomacy is also an important requirement.

Opportunities

Editorial work involves meeting composers and authors, and attending promotional functions such as conferences, exhibitions or media launches. The skills required are transferable, particularly to general book publishing.

Production controller

The job

When the editor has decided that the manuscript of a musical work or book on music is in its final version, with no further changes to be made, the manuscript is handed over to the production controller who supervises the process whereby the manuscript becomes the printed book or sheet of music ready for sale.

This process includes choosing a suitable music typesetter to turn the composer's manuscript into an accurate, attractive and clear version for the printer, which includes such details as ensuring that page turns are at a suitable place for instrumentalists and singers when they are performing. Typesetting is usually done on a computer using specially designed software. Simultaneously the production controller liaises with a designer to produce artwork for the cover. However, these functions in classical music publications are often dealt with by the editor and there is no separate production controller, except for the actual printing process: the costing, commissioning and control of print.

The production controller needs to decide on a suitable printer for the job – who may well be based in the Far East – and to advise on the type and thickness of paper to be used, and if necessary to order the appropriate quantity of paper required. The production controller may also need to oversee the production of recorded material such as CDs.

A most important part of the job is to supply the editors with an estimate of what it will cost to produce a particular title, and to make sure that those costs are not exceeded during the production process. Equally important is keeping to the publishing schedule, and ensuring that the right quality of publication is achieved.

Skills and abilities

A musical qualification may be required (preferably not highly specialized in one area). It is essential to have a logical approach to the job, and to be able to communicate well with a wide range of people. Any experience of printing is helpful. Training usually takes place as part of the job, but short courses are available on various aspects of the process.

Opportunities

The production controller will continually be acquiring the knowledge about advances in the technology of all aspects of publishing. A training in music and music book production would be a suitable background for posts in production departments in other types of publishing.

Advertising and sales promotion

The job

The main task is to promote the publisher's products and image by using advertising and sales promotion. This area controls the placing of advertisements in magazines, newspapers, etc., production of leaflets, posters, point-of-sale display material and – most important – product catalogues. The design and construction of exhibition stands and displays come within this area. Occasionally, an advertising agency may be used for the creative approach but usually this aspect is covered in-house.

Skills and abilities required

The most important requirements are an ability to work quickly and accurately under pressure to meet deadlines, an eye for detail and good communication skills. Employers will usually be looking for graduates, though not necessarily music graduates. It is important to be willing to use computers, data-bases and desk-top publishing. Good presentation and motivation are high priorities.

Opportunities

Gaining experience of sales promotion in music publishing could lead to filling a similar role in many other fields such as book publishing, publicity for arts festivals, or independent agency work for theatres or orchestras. Working for a magazine or journal is also a possibility.

Training

Many colleges and universities offer degree and postgraduate courses in publishing. However, a Diploma in Advertising from the CAM Foundation or in Marketing from the Institute of Marketing is very acceptable and can be obtained through part-time studies.

Music promotion (performances)

The job

This principally involves the introduction of the publisher's music catalogue to performers including orchestras, conductors, soloists, ensembles, festival and concert promoters, etc., recording companies and broadcasting companies. The object is to 'sell' a performance or recording for which the publisher and composer will receive a royalty (an important source of income). This position requires a high level of personal contact in the musical field.

Skills and abilities required

A good musical qualification, gained from one of the conservatoires or a university, is required (preferably not highly specialized in one area). A catholic taste in music would be an advantage, and also some fluency in a foreign language. An ability to communicate effectively both verbally and in writing is essential.

Opportunities

Music promotion involves meeting composers, performers, conductors and concert organizers at the highest level. Regular attendance at concerts, festivals and promotional functions is an important part of the job, as is travel within the UK and abroad.

Training

See the requirements for *Advertising and sales promotion* on **page 74**.

Hire librarian

The job

The hire library contains stocks of music from the publisher's repertoire not generally for sale, and includes orchestral sets, choral vocal scores and orchestral parts, opera scores and parts, musical plays and newly-commissioned works not yet published for sale. Customers include professional and amateur musicians, major and provincial orchestras, television and radio companies, recording companies, opera houses and choral societies. The hire librarian's task is to identify the customers' needs and to ensure that the correct material is supplied quickly and efficiently. The job also includes raising invoices, selecting music from stock, racking returned music, chasing overdue returns and seeking replacement of damaged and lost stock. The hire librarian's job requires a very sound knowledge of the publisher's catalogue, particularly new works. There is much direct customer contact, particularly by telephone and fax.

Skills and abilities required

Whilst a degree or equivalent in music is not essential, a sound knowledge of music (A-level or equivalent) is required. This post demands a methodical approach, accuracy, detail and the ability to work under pressure. Good inter-personal skills are essential for effective customer liaison, and an understanding of music-copying and/or printing is useful. A good general education is required, but on-the-job training is given. Again, fluency in a modern language may be useful.

Opportunities

Hire library work provides the chance to meet and deal with musicians and senior music administrators from all spheres. There may be opportunities to attend rehearsals and recording sessions, and the job offers the necessary experience and background for employment in orchestral libraries or related areas.

Sales representative

The job

The thrust is to sell sheet music and music books to music dealers, colleges and schools. The representative will generally work from home, covering a given geographical territory either in the UK or abroad, and will work to agreed sales targets. The job of the sales representative is to ensure that the music dealer is well stocked with the publisher's titles and that new titles are effectively marketed and stocked. Apart from direct selling on a day-to-day basis, representatives will also be involved in exhibitions, trade shows and workshops, when they will be talking to music dealers, professional and amateur musicians and members of the general public. The sales representative is also expected to provide a continuous feedback of information to the supervisor on competitive publishers' activities, changes in market demands and many other factors relating to the job.

Skills and abilities required

Self-motivation and an ability to communicate well with people, both verbally and in writing, are paramount. Selling skills are also essential, as is a current driving licence. Whilst a musical qualification is not necessary, a sound general knowledge of the subject would be useful (possibly to A level). A formal qualification in marketing and sales would be an advantage; for export sales, fluency in a modern language would also be helpful.

Opportunities

The job offers the opportunity to meet people in all areas of music, and also provides a sound training for sales representation in other industries, particularly general book publishing.

Training

Product knowledge training is given by the publisher. Many colleges offer courses leading to the Diploma in Marketing from the Institute of Marketing and candidates must meet the minimum entry requirements.

Copyright and other legal matters

These aspects are as important in a publishing house as they are for the performance and recording sectors referred to in *Working to help musicians* on **page 98**.

The job

This involves work on contracts and dealing with the registration and managing of copyrights, which may be done internationally or through a network of sub-publishers. It will be somebody's job to acquire rights and license these to bring maximum revenue (e.g. from performance, film and recordings). All this produces extensive data, which needs to be managed.

Skills and abilities required

You will not need a formal qualification in music to work in this area, but meticulous care and attention to detail, and skills in negotiating and communicating will be required. Familiarity with computers and the Internet will be important and some legal expertise would be very useful.

Opportunities and training

It may be possible to enter a publishing house at a junior level and work your way into this particular area through showing that you have the qualities required. There are degree and graduate courses in publishing and, increasingly in the music business, of Music Industry Management, where copyright and legal aspects are covered in modules or projects.

Other areas of employment

Some positions in publishing are common to many other commercial concerns and do not require a music qualification. Examples are shown in the chart on **page 78**:

GET A FOOTHOLD IN MUSIC PUBLISHING

Clerical Assistant required for busy small classical music publisher. Work includes orders, invoicing and photo-copying. Also answering customer queries, taking orders over the telephone and general office duties. Computer/ typing skills and the ability to work in a small team an advantage. Apply by letter, fax or e-mail with CV by Monday 29th July.

Printing	camera work and the use of new technology
Accountancy	financial management and credit control (Senior positions will require an accountancy degree, and more modest jobs a good general education.)
Computer operations	computer and programming and system work
Distribution	stock supervision, processing and packing

Useful addresses

- *British Phonographic Industry Ltd.,* 25 Savile Row, London W1X 1AA (telephone 0171 287 4422)
- *The Master Music Printers' and Engravers' Association,* 2–10 Plantation Road, Amersham, Buckinghamshire HP6 6HJ (telephone 01494 725525)
- *The Music Publishers' Association,* 3rd floor, Strandgate, 18–20 York Buildings, London WC2N 6JU (telephone 0171 839 7779)
- *The Music Retailers' Association,* PO Box 249, London W4 5EX (telephone 0181 994 7592)

Christine Wood, Music Education Editor, Oxford University Press

Musical instrument manufacture, maintenance and repair

The jobs

Design and construction: Modern and historical acoustic and electronic

Technical sales: Trade and retail (general or instrument specific), see *Sales* (page 82)

Servicing: Concert and domestic; musical and mechanical/electronic

Renovation/Restoration: Modern and antique (restoration/conservation)

Design and construction

Skills and abilities required

Craftworkers are single or multi-skilled in working a wide range of natural materials – especially wood, metals and plastics. Manual dexterity and speed skills are essential.

Electronic technicians/engineers need a good knowledge of audio electronics, PCB design and wiring skills.

Designers and makers/builders need a good depth of knowledge of the instrument users' requirements and a full range of construction/design skills. Management skills are also useful.

Opportunities

A few designers and a number of constructors are employed in the UK but the skills are in short supply in the world industry; the skills have the advantage of being universal and have changed little over decades.

Servicing

Skills and abilities required

Concert tuners, regulators/voicers (keyboard) need a high level of practical skill and experience in meeting the technical requirements of professional performance. They also need a high level of social skill and artistic appreciation.

Domestic tuner technicians (keyboard) need a good level of practical skill and resourcefulness. Some sales ability and good general musical and local knowledge are also required.

Instrument service technicians (electronic/wind/brass/string/percussion) need a high level of practical skill, knowledge and experience in servicing and regulating the above instruments to performers requirements.

Opportunities

Here the option is between working for an established business or self-employment. The established business will be the local dealer with a workshop or a large city showroom with a tuning/service connection. Work can either be in the showroom or workshop or outside in the concert hall or musician's home. In the past some people worked as tuners or technicians, but now most should be competent at both skills.

Self-employment as a tuner/technician is often chosen as a first step in starting a business as it requires high skill and knowledge but only a little capital. Sometimes a tuning/servicing connection can be purchased from a retiring tuner or subcontract work may be obtained from dealers.

Renovation/restoration (conservation)

Skills and abilities required

A good business can be based on domestic tuning and piano renovation, both of customers' instruments and also for resale.

The restoration and conservation of antique keyboard instruments is a new business developed over the last decades, with the increased awareness of historical instruments and early music. A good knowledge of the construction and technology of early instruments is necessary with practical skill and a good appreciation of the musical demands of players of 'early keyboards'. The renovation and restoration of electronic and acoustic non-keyboard instruments is an essential area of activity, both for modern and early instruments, to maintain the current stock in playing conditions.

Opportunities

Opportunities are as for servicing, either in established workshops or in the musician's own workshops on a self-employed basis. Conservation work is done mainly for museums or private collectors.

Training

General training

There are a few establishments that will accept apprentices and you should approach:

- the Crafts Council, 8 Waterloo Place, London SW1
- the Institute of Musical Instrument Technology, address below.

College courses

Some colleges offer full-time courses in instrument technology or repair, the majority of these being for two years, and leading to BTEC National or Higher National Diploma. Categories covered are not limited to keyboards; both early and modern fretted instruments, woodwind/brass and electronics may be found as a particular college's strength. There will often be compulsory studies in aspects of music history, theory and musical acoustics as they have a strong bearing on the construction of instruments.

Useful addresses – colleges

- *The Royal National College for the Blind,* College Road, Hereford HR1 1EB (telephone 01432 265725)
- *Merton College,* London Road, Morden, Surrey SM4 5QX (telephone 0181 640 3001
- *City of Leeds College of Music,* Cookridge Street, Leeds LS2 8BH (telephone 01532 452069/432491
- *Stevenson College of Further Education,* Bankhead Avenue, Sighthill, Edinburgh EH1 1DE (telephone 0131 535 4600)
- *West Dean College,* Chichester, West Sussex PO18 0QZ (telephone 01243 811301) – three year apprenticeship; renaissance and baroque, plucked and bowed instruments
- *London Guildhall University,* 41 Commercial Road, London E1 1LA (telephone 0171 320 1000/1845)
- *Newark and Sherwood College,* Friary Road, Newark, Nottinghamshire MG24 1PB (telephone 01636 705921)

If it is an important distinction for you at the time of entry to training, you may wish to enquire whether repair and maintenance, as opposed possibly to making, is the emphasis in a particular institution.

Other addresses – Trade Associations

- *Music Industries Association,* Grove Court, Hatfield Road, Slough, Berkshire SL1 1QU (telephone 01753 511550, fax 01753 539200)
- *Institute of Musical Instrument Technology,* 8 Chester Court, Albany Street, London NW1 4BU (telephone 0171 935 8682)
- *Pianoforte Tuners' Association,* 10 Reculver Road, Herne Bay, Kent CT6 6LD (telephone 01227 368808)

Terence M. Pamplin, Reader in Music Instrument Technology, London Guildhall University.

Sales

Retailing

The job

Music shops may sell instruments, accessories, music books and sheet music, recordings, or all of these.

Record shops may specialize in, for example, reggae or jazz, or may offer the whole spectrum of music. Some – but not so many – specialize in classical music. Local demand varies, and the shop manager must decide what to stock and must exercise tight stock control.

Music and instrument shops are not so widespread as record shops, and may hold a basic – or a very wide – selection of books and music; instruments can include the whole range of band and orchestral instruments, as well as guitars, pianos, electronic organs and keyboards. Electronic music equipment such as amplifiers and samplers tend to be found in specialist shops. 'Hire and Buy' schemes have become increasingly widespread, particularly for larger and more expensive instruments such as the piano, and some orchestral and band instruments.

Skills and abilities required

A high degree of musical skill is not essential, but it is obviously useful to be able to demonstrate various instruments, or replace a reed or a string. For selling pianos and other keyboards a reasonable level of ability to play is necessary, to demonstrate the difference between makes and models. With other instruments, such as guitars, a knowledge of the different accessories available is essential.

With sales of sheet music, a knowledge of different musical styles is very useful, as is awareness of music which is currently popular from film, television or major events.

Above all, what is required is:

- the ability to sell, and an interest in customers' needs
- numeracy (even though a calculator will assist you on hire and credit terms)
- a readiness to learn the business and find out about different manufacturers' and publishers' products
- an instinct for what products will sell, and how best to advertise them.

Opportunities and training

There is little training as such for the music retail trade. One way of starting is to enter a general retail training scheme, for example in a large department store. Music and record shops employ very few staff but a part-time job can sometimes lead to a full-time one. Recommendations by a relative or friend can be successful. Newspapers and specialist trade papers and magazines sometimes carry advertisements for vacancies. See also *Options to discuss with parents and staff: Leaving School at 16?* on **page 8**.

Trade sales

The retailer cannot operate without goods from the manufacturer. Here, sales people will not succeed without full appreciation of instrument technology, knowledge of the company's range and prices, and similarly those of the competition. So, selling and inter-personal skills (but with the 'business' rather than the public) and up-to-date market awareness will be priorities.

Most church and concert organs and harpsichords are sold directly to the user, so in the keyboard field the manufacturer-retailer connection is largely about pianos and electronic keyboards.

Music administration

Many people seek posts close to the practice of music. In small companies the employees may need to turn their hands to all aspects of the organization. It is not unknown in a small opera company, for example, for the administrator to put the music out, greet the guests and appear in the chorus in Act 2! In a larger concern you may have the chance to narrow the area of operations in terms of your responsibilities.

Here is an outline of the responsibilities and of the areas where you could find interesting work in music administration.

 London Symphony Orchestra
Resident at the Barbican

requires a committed

Education/ Access Assistant

To join the LSO's Discovery and Marketing teams.

Requirements are: one year's experience (minimum) in music administration; knowledge of music education practice; marketing and/or access experience; dtp skills preferred.

Salary according to experience; 9.30am – 6.00pm plus some evening work; 25 days annual leave; private healthcare; pension after one year's service.

For further information including job description, please contact the Discovery Department by phone (0171 588 1116) or fax (0171 374 0127).

Closing date for applications: 12 August 1996.

The LSO aims to be an equal opportunities employer.

The jobs

Artistic direction

- Extensive knowledge of repertoire and artists, producers, designers and other media experts
- Planning artistic policy, and programme content
- Lobbying for Arts Council and Lottery grants
- Medium and long-term strategy for development, including recordings and tours
- Commissioning, and new projects
- Vision

Press liaison, publicity and marketing

- VIP invitations, single and seasonal publicity
- Providing press and artists' followers with information and photographs
- Searching for reviews
- Writing or commissioning programmes, sleeve notes and biographies
- Assembling brochures, proofreading, liaison with printers, advertisers, and possible sponsors

Administration
- Often the first contact point for public and artists
- Booking halls, artists/conductors, travel arrangements, rehearsal venues, audition panels
- Supervising secretaries and computer operators
- Checking contracts, circulating work-schedules
- Keeping all the balls in the air on a day-to-day basis

Performance management
- Getting the performers onto the stage
- Checking music requirements with librarians/hire firms, and 'away' stage arrangements, seating, rostra
- Keeping list of extra players, instruments, singers, dancers
- Liaison with the Musicians' Union *et al*
- Liaison with hall staff

Venue management
- Some of the above in reverse
- Probably arrangement of hall's or local council's own events programme
- Liaison with other hirers, Health and Safety staff, VIP visitors
- Supervising ticket and catering arrangements
- Making the venue attractive and welcoming
- Balancing bookings of local groups with nationally-known artists

Agents and promoters

Their roles differ across styles of music, but agents generally seek gigs, tours and concert dates for their clients, while promoters take financial responsibility for presenting the event or series, taking the ticket and other sales income etc., on the assumption that the artists are famous enough to draw the crowds, or make an exciting debut. (Promotion is sometimes regarded as an aspect of publicity and marketing.)

See *Case study: Matthew* (**page 43**) and *Working to help musicians* (**page 98**).

The administrator

The job

All musicians, performers and composers deal with their own arrangements, engage the services of one or more specialists, or are part of an organization which has access to administrative expertise. All performing groups, amateur and professional as well as festivals, music associations, arts complexes, concert venues, music colleges, local authorities, music publishers, radio and television require skilled and competent organizers, often with a high level of knowledge and experience of music, although not necessarily trained as musicians. The title 'administrator' sounds bureaucratic and office-bound, but many in that role contribute creatively to the artistic enterprise.

Skills and abilities required

Good administrators should:

- 'never assume anything but remember everything'
- see the implications of courses of action
- sense in what order things need to be done (on a daily basis as well as medium and long-term).

The administrator must be sympathetic to the idiosyncratic needs of musicians, and be willing to operate as a member of a team. Depending upon the exact level of responsibility, the range of specializations in the administration and the size of the enterprise, the regular tasks of performing organizations tend to show a pattern, with many overlapping and linking responsibilities.

Opportunities

There are opportunities in large musical organizations such as symphony orchestras, opera houses and concert agencies as well as some pop bands. The Arts Council of England, Regional Arts Boards and the British Council have music officers with administrative functions. Broadcast and television companies, including independent stations and satellite channels, similarly have officers to administer music or, more broadly, arts services. Local councils and education authorities have staff whose responsibilities cover some of these functions. Posts in music colleges inevitably have a different emphasis, as the nature of the tutor-and-student relationship focuses the administrative work more sharply whilst covering many of the aspects shown. The concert hall management see the result of someone else's planning, but also need to frame an artistic policy, prevent clashes of repertoire, keep the environment attractive and control the box office and ticket availability.

See also *Appendix 1: Jobs in music advertised 1996* (**page 100**) – it shows a wide selection of responsibilities. The 'Creative and media' section in the *Guardian* on Mondays, *Classical Music* and *Arts Management Weekly* are good sources of information about vacancies.

Training

There are several courses in arts administration, found primarily at the universities of City (London), De Montfort in Leicester, Northumbria in Newcastle, Warwick, and East Anglia; also at Durham University Business School and Roehampton Institute. Some are postgraduate, some can be achieved part-time. They will not be specifically music-based.

Useful address

The Arts Council of England, 14 Great Peter Street, London SW1P 3NQ, runs many seminars and courses, and publishes consultation documents of national importance. Details are available from the Training Officer (telephone 0171 333 0100).

Case study: **Marcel: Getting into Arts administration**

Marcel enjoyed his time at Southend High School for Boys, and did Music at GCSE and A level, which he describes as 'a lonely experience' as he was the only one doing it. He moved on to Dartington College of Arts for a degree in Music and Arts Management with the latter as 'minor'. There was an emphasis on composing and performing, within a social context, looking at current issues in the arts; he also did a certain amount of studio recording. He decided to work in administration.

As part of the Dartington course he was able to secure an extended work experience of five weeks with Southend Borough Council Arts Department, setting up concerts and workshops. He also helped at the SE Essex Music Centre.

For some months he worked for Marks and Spencer (in a non-music capacity), and his job-seeking via the *Guardian* and *The Stage* was eventually rewarded. He gained a job as Arts Assistant (Music) with East Midlands Arts Board in Loughborough, and, at the time of writing, has been Acting Music Officer for some months.

Careers in TV and radio

The jobs

The jobs involve working – usually for a large enterprise – as a secretary, administrator, librarian, engineer, researcher, producer, editor, manager or performer. The post (with the probable exception of that of secretary) will almost certainly entail unsocial hours and presence may be required away from base. The high standards of British sound and vision media depend on expertise at all levels and the success of a live broadcast on radio or TV will be due to the fact that the preparation has been meticulous in all artistic and technical respects.

Pre-training may include areas such as hospital radio and student TV. You might be interested in the case study on Claire (*Getting into radio*, **page 90**).

Skills and abilities required

Some of the roles listed above are discussed briefly below.

Preparing a TV performance of a massive choral and orchestral piece in St Paul's Cathedral on the one hand and a jazz programme for radio on the other would seem to require a number of differing abilities. However, in **production and direction** terms the purely musical judgements to be exercised would be similar. Directors are responsible for creative decisions which make the final programme. Producers have a strong artistic input but also need planning ability, general music awareness, ability to make discriminating appraisal of performance standards, technical and financial knowledge and an imaginative approach to broadcasting.

Public service organizations such as the BBC hold attractions for musicians in the areas of both sound engineering and programme-making but there is need to accept the strong studio-based no-audience-present nature of some of the music performance work. Many local and independent radio stations make a considerable contribution to the provision of a wide range of music, catering for a large listening public with very few staff. As with their larger counterparts, they may preview, broadcast and review all styles of live performances, sustain numerous discussions on air (at and away from base) and play a host of recordings. In some posts related to **presentation** in radio and television, the ability to write succinctly will be necessary. One source of advice states that voice, intelligence and qualifications, followed by the ability to read from autocue (TV), ad lib and interview people confidently are the core skills for fronting programmes.

An experienced **studio manager** (radio) will need artistic and technical ability to produce a balanced sound. **Editing** (choosing which of various takes give the best sequence for transmission) may be done by an assistant. A **floor manager** (TV) will interpret and relay the producer's requirements to those people working on the set. The programme can have hundreds of performers or only one.

Opportunities

Many senior production posts in the large organizations are filled by internal promotion. Sound and vision media will always want to recruit at a high level from other specialisms e.g. journalism, and music is an area where specialist experience outside broadcasting can be advantageous. It could be that at **assistant producer** and **researcher** level this will be a useful commendation. All organizations need excellent secretarial and administrative support and it may be possible to move from that area to production assistantship.

As the shape of the broadcasting industry changes, more work is done for large enterprises by freelancers and outside contractors. You can see this from the information at the end of credits after a TV programme. This means that fewer salaried positions now exist. Since their inception, Independent Television and Channel 4 have produced and broadcast many excellent music programmes while working on different bases, e.g. having no permanent orchestras, and some companies having no head of music. Again, much more 'buying-in' of performance is therefore necessary for series arrangements as well as for single events. The number of full time posts in television concerned predominantly with serious music is probably only a dozen or so.

Other changes involve challenges to established procedures, for example the competition between Classic FM and BBC Radio 3. These involve decisions about how best to deliver broadcast classical music, whether explanatory talk is required and in what style.

The Internet is a vast world of information, and the installation of Integrated Systems Digital Network (ISDN) means that some concerts from major venues can be heard live by net surfers. Vision will probably go down the same line shortly. Copyright is a factor in all this.

Training

Much depends on whether your interest is sound engineering or music/arts production; both are referred to in other sections of this book (**pages 92–95**). The large corporations can take entrants at both degree and other levels. ITV publishes the *ITV Careers Handbook*, priced at about £10 (ITV Centre, 200 Gray's Inn Road, London WC1X 8XZ) and the BBC offers a free brochure, *The Way In*, through its BBC Recruitment Services, PO Box 7000, London W5 2WY.

This is a very competitive job market. Skillset, the industry training body for broadcast, film and video, has indicated that from over 30,000 student places for Media Studies in further and higher education, probably only about 500 will achieve entry to TV production grade training. In 1995, the BBC received 80,000 enquiries about broadcasting, but took in only 2100 people at all levels. About 5000 apply for journalism and studio management training but probably not more than ten would be successful in each case.

Case study: **Claire: Getting into radio**

My enthusiasm for music goes back to my primary school days, when I learned recorder, clarinet and, later, piano. I had an opportunity through a composition competition to visit Radio Cambridgeshire's studios soon after moving to secondary school and this really caught my interest. Later, although concentrating on my (11) GCSEs, I used my work experience to assist in a live recording of Selwyn College Choir in their Chapel in Cambridge.

I had kept up my playing (including alto saxophone for my County Wind Band), and was pleased that a composition of mine was used in a published GCSE Music guide. A-level subjects and degree choices then caused some problems as I wanted to combine my interests and take Music Technology at 18+, but soon found the Physics a struggle. Music, French and History became the combination.

After GCSEs I enjoyed a week's more formal work experience with local radio, and volunteered to go in and answer phones etc., at weekends and holidays. This soon became paid work and gave more valuable training ranging from Newsroom Production Assistant to Gram Librarian, so I could confidently fill in for staff.

Having applied for various HE courses including those with a Music Technology bias, I was eventually accepted – although my A levels did not go quite as planned! – by Anglia (then a polytechnic), after taking the precaution of sounding out one or two retake possibilities. I revelled in the Anglia course, spent a great deal of time playing and singing (including being in the chorus for *Peter Grimes* and playing in Stravinsky's Octet) and chaired the Music Students' Committee. The course gave several choices and I became very interested in Arts Administration by way of Law, Marketing and Finance modules.

After an overall 2:1 degree classification, I very nearly stayed on for a postgraduate MA in composition, but decided to postpone this and cannot be sure that I will take it up. Teaching was also a possibility, and I have fortunately been able to continue a small amount of Saturday morning instrumental teaching taken on during college days.

My local radio let me return for the summer after the Anglia degree, but I still hadn't a 'proper job' so set out on the applications trail. Trying to combine my interests and experiences attractively, I applied for 13 posts, including:

> Concerts Administrator, Publicity Officer, Clarinet Teacher, Radio posts as Gram Librarian, and Production Assistant (some BBC posts are advertised only internally).

From the 13 applications, I had five interviews, and the only one I was offered was Assistant, Radio 3 Publicity for BBC (full-time) initially on a six-month contract, now permanent. I am benefiting a great deal from the in-house training, latterly in writing for broadcasting.

Virtually all the experience gained in the practical area of broadcasting has come through persuading local radio studios to let me work part-time at holidays and weekends, rather than through traditional school-based studies. However, I think that a wide range of school and area music-making, plus a degree that fitted my needs very well, were also very helpful in getting me to the five interviews.

Working in recording studios

The job

Basic tasks around the studio might include going to the shop to buy some sockets, preparing the cabling, microphones and control apparatus for recording. Maintenance of equipment may also be required in a small studio, and/or assistance with mobile recording gear. Junior staff will find themselves fulfilling these tasks for some time, and the hours are decidedly unsocial. Large enterprises will have more than one studio, 48-track digital and analogue facilities. Some offer sound duplication; some will record at location. A few will transcribe from old recordings. Entry as a trainee may be as early as 16, but you will need to apply more than once to coincide with a vacancy. Life is hard at the bottom end of this sector of employment, but there can be pleasures of interesting locations and work with famous artists.

Skills and abilities required

The ideal candidate has boundless enthusiasm, interest, adaptability, common sense and a knowledge of which 'takeaways' are still open at 3.00 a.m. Studio staff need to deal cheerfully with all sorts of crises and temperaments. More than a working knowledge of computer operations is desirable. The job on the lowest rung is usually a studio assistant. Promotion brings specific requirements of accurate loading, timing and monitoring of controls, and probably also requires competence to repair some of the equipment.

Opportunities

This is an area in which setting up on one's own may be considered at some stage, but gaining expertise and experience in an established company will usually precede this.

If you find yourself in one of the 20 or so large studios, the plusses will include:

- working your apprentice time with many experienced and specialist practitioners

- operating, even in a modest way, with eminent musicians across the whole spectrum of music
- access to the newest technology.

If you work in a smaller business, there will be:

- experience in a broad range of duties, and responsibility much earlier, and therefore possibly, the chance to influence the firm's policy
- a feeling that your talents are not lost within a large enterprise.

Progression after the early years is to **sound mixer**, or fully-fledged **balance engineer**, and the higher echelons of management and production. Titles for posts may vary. Experienced and successful engineers develop strong associations with particular artists and therefore become sought after outside their main studio, or even when working with other 'labels'.

Training

The recording studios in the country are numbered in hundreds but many studio engineer/technicians work freelance. Almost all training is 'on the job'. However, a number of further education colleges offer BTEC ND in Music Technology and some offer HND. Many universities now offer courses that lead to recognized qualifications in recording/technology. Entry requirements can be demanding – Maths, Physics and Music A levels may be required for some courses.

Two other points

- Recording technology continues to advance rapidly; it is not always the case that even digital audio tape is used (**NB** the links with music technology and composing).
- However well qualified you are, it's your personality and ability that are crucial factors.

The record business

General

Unless you are intending a degree-level entry, you may need to find a junior post and work your way to an arm of the company that attracts you. As suggested elsewhere, working in music retail can be a useful entrée. You can see how marketing and promotion work from a different angle, and their effect on the buying public.

There are usually about 150 record companies in business at any one time, and they may account for 15 per cent of personnel in the wider music business. Major international firms such as EMI jostle with smaller independents ('indies') and specialists. All watch the sales trends keenly. One Britpop group sold nearly 350,000 copies of a hit in one week. Album (CDs, cassettes and LPs) deliveries to all outlets were over 200 million for the 12 months to March 1996.

The jobs

Cassettes and CDs need selling. In the popular fields, **pluggers** will use a variety of strategies to build up good relations with DJs and those who influence the radio stations' play lists, and thus sales and the charts. A town record shop may receive up to ten visits a week from sales people dealing in singles. Other aspects of **promotion** of all recordings include liaison with journalists, reviewers, magazines, design of – and text for – posters, sleeves and notes and an efficient distribution section. The advertising of recordings is a whole world of its own.

Video production is yet another area of promotion and marketing requiring an imaginative eye for the additional visual, theatrical and lighting effects. As for television, both a producer and director are involved. Overlapping techniques are required for making a video of a production, for example from an opera house. There is also a developing market in CD ROMs, and soon likely to be in Digital Video Discs (DVD).

Returning to recordings, **sound engineers** (who in the classical field may need a music degree or equivalent) have the critical task of preparing the studio, or location, microphones, control desk and all aspects of hardware and software to optimum working conditions. **Producers** will probably spend a good deal of time with artists before and after the recording and will then decide exactly what type of sound is required, dealing with balance between musicians, fixing the order of takes – in short, taking responsibility for the actual master produced, with artistic judgement involved. So that the artists can give their best performance, the producer and **balance engineer** need to do work in close harmony. Either may **edit**.

None of this can happen unless the artist has been signed up with the company. The Artists and Repertoire person (**A and R**) has the creative but not always enviable task of seeking out talent, fending off the not-so-talented and making sense of artist availability, accompaniment, venue, live performance and tour tie-in to best advantage. This can be a heady mixture of creative ideas and realistic execution.

Record-making is a very big business. Not every aspect of its future is assured – piracy has to be eradicated, classical sales have had a tendency to plateau, and subscription 'on-line' availability is very likely – but it's an exciting field to be in, even with its decidedly anti-social hours.

Roadies and orchestral attendants

The job

The essential people who perform the more physically strenuous support functions for jazz, rock and pop bands seem simply to have different titles from those who work for orchestras and larger bands. The *Administration* section (**pages 84–87**) shows that various responsibilities overlap between designated jobs – likewise here, some music management tasks below cross over into those of roadie, porter and attendant. Even assuming that the pre-concert planning has been done, and all front-of-house work is covered, somebody has to check:

- that the stage requirements, including dimensions, dressing rooms and special rostra are as ordered, and there are no particular restrictions
- that lighting, heating and power, sound and public address systems are working
- that instruments are transported safely at all times, and loaded and unloaded from van and stage (This requires specialist care and physical resilience – for example, do any harps have to be taken up spiral staircases?)
- the sequence of groups in the performance schedule – particularly important in clubs and pubs
- that the audience is not uncomfortably near the performers and that the latter are not operating in dangerous conditions
- whether physical arrangements for any TV, photographers or recordings restrict performers' movement
- who stays in attendance during the performance (important with school performing groups *et al*)
- whether equipment needs to be hired or returned before the next gig or concert
- the arrangements for security of instruments in a venue, in transit to the next job and at all stopping places, especially on foreign tours
- who is driving a) the equipment, b) the performers away from the current performance – in either case this may be the roadies or attendants themselves
- who is responsible for waking up the band for the next day's work
- particularly abroad, whether there will be large temperature fluctuations during the day and evening and efficient air-conditioning.

Skills and abilities required

Primarily, both functions require physical resilience, a knack of getting on with people, and virtues of diplomacy and flexibility. Inconvenient hours are worked. In some large rock and pop bands, specific knowledge of guitar, amplifier and keyboard repairs will be required, together with a stock of accessories. Understanding the needs of recording studios and technicians is helpful to all groups mentioned here. The band roadie may have to live with the difficulties of short-term engagements and no security of tenure.

Opportunities

There is a chance of progression to management (or a bigger group which has a better van and pays a more generous retainer fee between concerts and tours!).

Working to help musicians

There are several jobs that involve providing assistance to musicians and music organizations. The **artists' agencies** and **professional associations** are most directly involved with the careers, and conditions of work of musicians, the former being critical to success in attracting employment. Keen sensitivity to musicians' needs, particularly those of the newly trained, and a talent for keeping clients in the eye of the appropriate 'target group' are essential attributes. The top-line agency may specialize but should operate as successfully for the new graduate as for the internationally-renowned star performer. The professional associations tread an unenviable path between proper demands for reasonable reimbursement and conditions, and the employers' needs to run their organizations with a fair eye to financial viability as well as artistic vision.

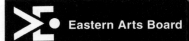

Eastern Arts Board

Eastern Arts Board is the arts funding and development agency for the East of England. Its mission is to enrich the quality of life in the Eastern region by fostering and developing the arts. It is the fastest growing region in the country with new and vibrant leadership. It has arts organisations and the excitement of being at the centre of the region's The Year of Opera and Musical Theatre 1997.

Music Officer

To contribute to, and carry out the Board's policy for the development of music throughout the region and bring specialist knowledge and experience to departmental and Board policies as a whole.

Experience of strategic planning and relevant arts management experience is important, as is a willingness to work as part of a team in the Performing Arts Department.

The Incorporated Society of Musicians (ISM) also has an important education section which relates to LEAs and organizes valuable one-day conferences. The Musicians Union (MU) supports interesting ventures such as the English Northern Philharmonia training scheme (see *Professional orchestras*, **page 33**).

With rather less direct involvement but very important to musicians are **accountants** and **instrument insurers**. The accountant can act only on information given by the artist in terms of, for example, what might legitimately be claimed as expenses, but needs an understanding of the peculiar life musicians lead and the unusual ways in which they are paid. The instrument insurers will probably be an insurance person first and a musician second but it is helpful to acknowledge the many situations in which artists need protection against accidents, temperature variations, travel abnormalities, let alone Third Party, Fire and Theft. One firm – British Reserve is an example – might concentrate on 'classical' instruments and secure the greater part of that particular sector of the market. Another might offer more package arrangements for groups including road insurance and diversification into related activities as well, possibly requiring more musical knowledge from some of its staff.

A very large, essentially music-based institution such as an opera house may employ over 200 staff within its total payroll who do not need musical knowledge as such. But one example might be a **translator**, who works freelance, and can also be available for work on orchestra programme notes or correspondence and faxes about an extensive foreign tour. Another might be a **language coach**.

Firms which specialize in equipment hire (instruments, sound control, staging etc.) are important to the music business.

There is always a need for a particular kind of musical expertise in a major **auction house** which holds specialist instrument sales and offers a valuation service. (A different figure may be realized for an instrument in an auction from that for which it has been insured.) So, knowledge of 'the trade' is vital, together with a deep respect for craftsmanship and understanding of the history of instruments. There may occasionally be vacancies in specialist music booksellers.

The important areas of **copyright** are supervised by such organizations as the Performing Rights Society (PRS) and the Mechanical Copyright Protection Society (MCPS). The PRS protects the interests of composers where music is performed in public bars, hotel corridors and jukeboxes as well as concert halls. It distributed £167 million to 28,000 members in 1995. It employs 650 people and supports a number of 'Composer in Education' schemes. The MCPS employs 300 people and distributed £137.4m to composers and publishers in 1995. It protects the interests of both when copyright musical works are recorded. Phonographic Performance Ltd (PPL) similarly administers public performance and broadcasting rights on behalf of record labels. These organizations will have posts in the areas of data collection, negotiation, licensing, the establishment of copyright and the maintenance of discographies and libraries.

Musical organizations will need to have in-house, or to use on a freelance basis, professionals in:

- public and media relations
- marketing and advertising
- travel for music groups (including foreign tours)
- equipment hire.

Busy individual musicians may need to buy in help in:

- diary bookings
- instrument repairs
- specialist medical support.

Appendix 1: Jobs in music advertised 1996

Note: This list does not include teaching and performance posts.

PA to Head of Music	BBC Worldwide Publishing
Sales Assistants (p/t)	English National Opera
Licensing Administrator	Decca Record Company
Office Assistant/Administrator	Monteverdi Choir and Orchestra
Production Assistant	*Classic CD* Magazine
Business Organizer	BBC Proms
Community Youth Development Co-ordinator	National Youth Music Theatre
Secretary /Administrator	Dixon, Music Industry Accountants
Artists and Recording Editor	*Music Week*
Administrator/Manager	Music at Oxford
Marketing Assistant	Yamaha-Kemble UK, Milton Keynes
Arts/Education Practitioner	English National Opera
Curator	The Elgar Birthplace Trust
Recording Manager	Royal Northern College of Music
Administrator	Friends of the LSO
Editor	*Music News Asia*
Bass or baritone	Opera North
Editorial Assistant	*The Strad*
Concerts Administrator	Manchester Bridgewater Hall (new international concert venue)
Head of Planning	Royal Scottish National Orchestra
Sales Administrator	Boosey and Hawkes
Mail Order Supervisor	Boosey and Hawkes
Assistant Editor	*Guitar* magazine
Administrative Director (p/t)	The Early Music Network
Director	British Music Information Centre
Secretary/PA in vocal division	IMG Artists Agency
Experienced Music Librarian	London Philharmonic Orchestra
Assistant Literary Manager	English National Opera
Assistant (Company Development)	Pimlico Opera
Production Planner (CD & vinyl)	Mayking Multi-Media
Development Manager	English National Opera
Secretary/Receptionist	Royal College of Organists
Receptionist/Telephonist(p/t)	Associated Board of RSM
Personal Manager	for International conductor
Trainee Cataloguer	Sotheby's auctioneers, Collectors' Dept. Rock and Roll
Events Co-ordinator	Philharmonic Hall, Liverpool
Information/Education Co-ordinator	Women in Music

Head of Vocal Studies	Guildhall SM&D
Secretary to the Director of Music	Guildhall SM&D
Head of Development	Opera North, Leeds
Marketing Manager	English National Opera
Administrator Baylis programme	English National Opera (Education Outreach)
Marketing Officer	Welsh National Orchestra, Cardiff
Administrator Music & Drama	North West Arts Board, Manchester
Administrative Director (p/t)	Leicester International Music Festival
Several new posts	Liverpool Institute of Performing Arts
Director	Britten-Pears School for Advanced Musical Studies (Aldeburgh)
Music Assistant and Radio 3 Promotions Assistant	BBC Philharmonic, Manchester
Personal Assistant	Film Composer London
General Manager	London Concert Choir
Membership Assistant	Friends of Covent Garden (Royal Opera House)
Promotion/Sales person	JW Media Music, London
Marketing Manager	Eastern Orchestral Board
Marketing Assistant	Halle Orchestra
Head of Fund-raising	Royal Opera House
Clerical Assistant	Stainer and Bell (music publisher)
External Relations Assistant	City of Leeds College of Music
Accounts Executive	Warner Music UK
Music Producer, TV/Media	Boosey & Hawkes
PA to the Administrator	National Opera Studio
Asst. to Personnel Manager	London Symphony Orchestra
Education/Access Assistant	London Symphony Orchestra
Senior Production Manager	English National Opera (ENO)
Head of Corporate Giving, Orchestra Manager	City of Birmingham Symphony Orchestra
Sheet Music Sales Assistant	Music Shop, London SW
Licensing Officer	Phonographic Performance Ltd
Marketing Officer	BBC Symphony Orchestra
Development Director (funding)	Northern Sinfonia, Newcastle
Community Education Officer	Opera North, Leeds
Operations Manager (Tours)	Specialised Travel
Education Manager	English Touring Opera
General Manager (part-time)	London Concert Choir
Music Mad Marketing Officer	The Stables, Milton Keynes (John Dankworth/Cleo Laine)
Sponsorship Assistant	City of Birmingham Symphony Orchestra
General Manager	The Sixteen (small professional choir)
Press Officer (Classical Music)	Barbican Centre

Head of Publications	English National Opera
Music Repertoire Manager	Oxford University Press
Operational Engineer (Classical Location Recording)	Decca Record Company
Assistant to Sales Manager	Omnibus Press (Popular Music books)
Publicity Officer	Scottish Chamber Orchestra
Sponsorship Assistant	City of Birmingham Symphony Orchestra
Administrative Assistant	SPNM/Sonic Arts Network
Education Officer	London Philharmonic Orchestra
Development Officer	London Philharmonic Orchestra
Receptionist	Major West London recording studio
Full time sales staff (Garage, House, Soul, Hip)	Uptown Records, London WI
Music Director	Southend Boys' Choir
Secretary, Music Department	Morley College, London SE1
Prop Maker	English National Opera
Full-time Assistant	The Musicians' Diary Service
Sales/Promotion Copywriter	Music Sales Group
Choral Animateur	City of Coventry Performing Arts
Press and Promotions Officer	Carlton Classics
Marketing Manager	Glasgow Royal Concert Hall
Music Officer	Eastern Arts Board
Orchestra Librarian	City of Birmingham Symphony Orchestra
Administrator	Guitar Institute
Marketing Assistant	National Youth Orchestra (Bristol)
Foyer Music Co-ordinator	Royal Festival Hall
Assistant Music Officer	Leeds City Leisure Services
Co-ordinator	Community Music East (Norwich)
Marketing Manager	National Centre for Popular Music (Sheffield)
Concerts Assistant	London Sinfonietta
Assistant Managing Editor	*BBC Music* Magazine
Administrator (part-time)	Live Music Now, South West.
Brass Tuner/Inspector	Boosey and Hawkes

Note

The advertisements and the log of vacant posts are real examples. However, all the vacancies will have been filled before the publication of this book.

Appendix 2: Some additional notes

- In a survey on youth participation in the Arts, three-quarters of respondents said that they had enjoyed their arts experiences at both primary and secondary stages. Those who had become involved said that there were positive outcomes such as personal and social development (getting on with people and feeling more confident), and greater insights and awareness. (*Source: National Foundation for Educational Research.*)
- At both GCSE and A level, the percentage of candidates with successful grades at A* to C (previously A–C) are consistently well above the average for all subjects. Numbers of music candidates at GCSE rose from 27,577 in 1988 to 41,801 in 1996. A-level entries have also been rising, from 5509 in 1993 to 6518 in 1996.
- The Royal National Institute for the Blind (RNIB) and the Music Publishers' Association have produced a handbook called *Music in large print*. It deals with availability of enlarged copies through purchase or photocopying, and copyright, and costs about £3 plus postage. Contact RNIB (telephone 0181 968 8600).
- Five per cent of London's labour force is employed in the Arts and related manufacturing industries. Well over 2000 music businesses in the city employ close to 30,000 people. (*Source: London Arts Board.*)
- 'There are *explorers* and there are *obsessives*. The first may take some time to bring together – and exploit – a wide range of experiences in music posts. The second have ... clearly defined goals like "film music composer" or "baroque oboist" and sometimes have to come to terms with compromises which do not invalidate their original intention.'

  Andrew Peggie in *Music Scholar* (Rhinegold Publishing Ltd), March 1996

- CATS stands for Credit Accumulation and Transfer Scheme, which allows a degree to be awarded on completion of 360 credits (120 at each of three levels). The scheme is helpful if a personal difficulty or severe illness requires a transfer of institution.
- The Music Publishers Association (MPA) – address in *Music publishing*, **page 78** – offers an interesting service to others in the music publishing industry. People seeking posts may lodge their CVs, in a particular format, with the MPA who will then circulate a list to employers from time to time. While offering this helpful facility, the MPA cannot act as job-finder, or be active beyond passing job-seekers' information on.
- Rock School Ltd has initiated a series of graded examinations validated by Trinity College, London. Its address is: Broomfield House, Broomfield Road, Kew Gardens, Surrey TW9 3HS (telephone 0181 332 6303).

Appendix 3: Useful addresses

AKLOWA, Takely House, Brewer's End, Takely, Bishop's Stortford, CM22 6QR (telephone 01279 871 062)

Arts and Entertainment Training Council, 3 St Peter's Buildings, York Street, Leeds LS9 8AJ (telephone 0113 244 8845) – AETC is the leading body developing standards of competence for occupations in the performing arts, relevant to vocational qualifications.

Associated Board of the Royal Schools of Music, 14 Bedford Square, London WCLB 3JG (telephone 0171 636 5400)

Association of Professional Composers, 34 Hanway Street, London WlP DE (telephone 0171 436 0919)

Association of Professional Music Therapists, 38 Pierce Lane, Fulbourn, Cambridgeshire CB1 5DL (telephone 01223 880377)

Association of Professional Recording Services (APRS) 2 Windsor Square, Silver Street, Reading, Berkshire RG1 2TH (telephone 01734 756218)

Bhavan Centre, 4A Castletown Road, London W14 9HQ (telephone 0171 81 3086)

Black Music Industry Association, 146 Manor Park Road, London NW10 4JP (telephone 0181 961 4857)

British Federation of Young Choirs, 37 Frederick Street, Loughborough LE11 3BH

British Library National Sound Archive, 29 Exhibition Road, London W7 (telephone 0171 412 7440)

British Music Information Centre, 10 Stratford Place, London WlM 9AE (telephone 0171 499 8567)

British Phonographic Industry (BPI), 25 Savile Row, London, WlX 1AA (telephone 0171 287 4422)

British Society for Music Therapy, 25 Rosslyn Avenue, E Barnet, Hertfordshire EN4 8DH (telephone 0181 368 8879)

British Youth Opera, 103 Borough Road, London SE1 OAA (telephone 0171 815 6090/93)

Careers and Occupational Information Centre (COIC), PO Box 298A, Thames Ditton, Surrey KT7 OZS (telephone 0181 957 5030)

Composers' Guild, 34 Hanway Street, London WlP 9DE (telephone 0171 436 0007)

English Folk Dance and Song Society, 2 Regents Park Road, London NWI 7AY (telephone 0171 485 2206)

Graduate Teacher Training Registry (GTTR), Fulton House, Jessop Avenue, Cheltenham, Gloucestershire GL50 3SH (telephone 01242 225868)

Incorporated Society of Musicians (ISM), 10 Stratford Place, London WlN 9AE (telephone 0171 629 4413)

Jazz Services Ltd, 5 Dryden Street, London WC2E 9NW (telephone 0171 829 8352–4)

Mechanical-Copyright Protection Society, Elgar House, 41 Streatham High Road, London SW16 1ER (telephone 0181 664 4400)

Music For Youth (National Festival and Schools' Prom), 4 Blade Mews, London SW15 2NN (telephone 0181 870 9624)

Musicians' Union, 60–62 Clapham Road, London SW9 OJJ (telephone 0171 82 5566)

National Association for Music Education (NAME, formerly MANA), 52 Hall Orchard Lane, Frisby-on-the-Wreake, Melton Mowbray, Leicestershire LE14 2NH (telephone 01664 434379)

National Music Council, Francis House, Francis Street, London SW1P 1DE (telephone 0181 347 8618)

National School Band Association, 52 Hall Orchard Lane, Frisby-on-the-Wreake, Melton Mowbray, Leicestershire LE14 2NH (telephone 01664 434379)

National Youth Brass Band of Great Britain, 85 Uvedale Road, Enfield, Middlesex EN2 6HD (telephone 0181 482 0354)

National Youth Choir of Great Britain, PO Box 67, Holmfirth, Huddersfield HD7 1GQ (telephone 01484 687 023)

National Youth Jazz Association, 11 Victor Road, Harrow, Middlesex A2 6PT (telephone 0181 863 2717)

National Youth Music Theatre, 2 Bow Street, London WC2E 7BA (telephone 0171 836 9791)

National Youth Orchestra of Great Britain, 32 Old School House, Britannia Road, Bristol BS15 2DB (telephone 0117 960 0477, NYO Scotland 0141 332 8311, NYO Wales 01222 561231)

Performing Rights Society (PRS), 29–33 Berners Street, London WlP 4AA (telephone 0171 580 5544)

Phonographic Performance Ltd (PPL), Ganton House, 14–22 Ganton Street, London WlV 1LB (telephone 0171 437 0311)

Pro Corda (Young Chamber Music Players), Leiston Abbey House, Theberton Road, Leiston, Suffolk IP16 4TB (telephone 01728 831354)

Rhinegold Publishing (Music Yearbooks, Classical Music etc.), 241 Shaftesbury Avenue, London WC2H 8EH (telephone 0171 333 1721)

Sing for Pleasure, 25 Fryerning Lane, Ingatestone, Essex CM4 ODD (telephone 01277 353691 (Day and residential courses for young singers)

UCAS, PO Box 67, Cheltenham, Gloucestershire GL50 3SA (telephone 01242 222444)

WOMAD, Mill Lane, Box, Nr. Corsham, Wilts SN13 8PN (telephone 01225 743 188)

Young Concert Artists Trust, 23 Garrick Street, London WC2E 9AX (telephone 0171 379 8477)

Young Musicians' Symphony Orchestra, Flat 4, Gunnersbury Avenue, London W5 3NJ (telephone 0181 993 3135)

Youth and Music, 28 Charing Cross Road, London WC2H ODB (telephone 0171 379 6722) – operates *Stagepass,* a nationwide ticket concessionary scheme for young people

Conservatoires

Birmingham Conservatoire (faculty of the University of Central England in Birmingham), Paradise Place, Birmingham B3 3HG (telephone 0121 331 5901/2)

City of Leeds College of Music, Cookridge Street, Leeds LS2 8BH (telephone 0113 243 2491)

Guildhall School of Music and Drama, Silk Street, Barbican, London EC2Y 8DT (telephone 0171 628 2571)

London College of Music at Thames Valley University, St. Mary's Road, Ealing, London W5 5RF (telephone 0181 231 2304/2692)

Royal Academy of Music, Marylebone Road, London NW1 5HT (telephone 0171 873 7373)

Royal College of Music, Prince Consort Road, London SW7 2BS (telephone 0171 589 3643)

Royal Northern College of Music, 124 Oxford Road, Manchester M13 9RD (telephone 0161 273 6283)

Royal Scottish Academy of Music and Drama, 100 Renfrew Street, Glasgow G2 3DB (telephone 0141 332 4101)

Trinity College of Music, 11–13 Mandeville Place, London WlM 6AQ (telephone 0171 935 5773)

Welsh College of Music and Drama, Castle Grounds, Cathays Park, Cardiff CF1 3ER (telephone 01222 342854/640054)